Glowing endorsements for *Kenn Blanchard*

"Rev. Kenn Blanchard turns the common stereotypes of race, guns and gun control from upside down to right side up! He brilliantly flips the tables on the politically correct lies of the anti-gun political establishment and liberal media machine by bringing the urban black shooter out of the shadows and into the mainstream with the rest of America's law-abiding gun owners. I'm damn proud to call him a friend!"

Mark Walters
Host of Armed American Radio
Co-author *Lessons from UNarmed America*

"Kenn Blanchard has been one of the leading voices for Second Amendment rights for decades. His new book, *Black Man WIth A Gun: Reloaded*, bucks stereotypes and challenges political leaders who want to disarm African Americans using gun-control laws left over from per Civil War era. The Rev. Blanchard devotes his life to empowering the black community to defend themselves with both weapons of war and the shield of Christ. This book is a must-read for all those who need the facts and insights to arm themselves in the fight for the rights to keep and bear arms."

– Emily Miller, Senior Editor of Opinion,
The Washington Times
Author, *Emily Gets Her Gun*

"A born protector, this Marine turned cop turned preacher knows our history and why self-defense is a fundamental, natural right. From the pulpit to the halls of Congress, Kenn has spoken up for all of us, even if we weren't paying attention. *Black Man with a Gun: Reloaded* is an excellent resource for the new shooter and a true history lesson on the struggle for all people to be free."

– Richard Johnson, *www.BlueSheepdog.com*

Glowing endorsements for *Kenn Blanchard*

"I first met Kenn several years ago. I was a white man with a gun, Kenn was a black man with a gun. It was quite literally a divine appointment as in addition to our work in helping secure our nation from those who would do it harm, we discovered a mutual love for the Lord and a calling to ministry. Kenn and I soon began leading a weekly Bible study for others where we worked and our friendship grew. Kenn is one of the most genuine people I have ever met; no arrogance, just a sincere love for God, family, seeing lives changed, and a dedication to protecting the freedoms our Constitution guarantees but are so often under attack. I'm proud to call him a friend and a patriot."

> – Doug Gilmer, a.k.a The Backcountry Chaplain,
> *www.BackcountryChaplain.com*

"In *Black Man with a Gun: Reloaded*, Reverend Kenn Blanchard reveals unspoken truths about race, religion, fatherhood, and more. In this new book the Reverend lets us examine the complex forces that contend for his soul: a Christian minister; a government agent who travelled the world protecting our freedom; a disarmed civilian; a committed husband and father; a Black Man; a Black; a Man. Reverend Kenn wrestles with memories of his own father, lays bare his encounters with racism, and demonstrates friendship, loyalty, commitment and love on his journey. You need not be Black, male, armed, or even a supporter of the Second Amendment to appreciate *Black Man with a Gun: Reloaded*; in the end, it is about America. It is about us."

> Rabbi Dovid Bendory, Rabbinic Director, Jews for the
> Preservation of Firearms Ownership

Black Man with a Gun:

RELOADED

Kenn
Blanchard

Foreword

The first time I met Kenn Blanchard, he was wandering through the bookstore tables at the Gun Rights Policy Conference in 2007. He was clearly startled that I recognized him and knew his name. He was even more startled when he realized who I was and that my father, gun rights legend Neal Knox, was a fan of his work. I bought another copy of *Black Man with a Gun* right there on the spot and asked him to sign it for me. I wanted the signed copy because I knew the importance of the book and that Kenn was destined for great things – time has proven me right, and the promise continues to build.

Reverend Kenn is one of the most thoughtful, calm, and reasoned voices in the gun debate. His compassion and commitment shine through in everything he does, and his unique perspective, as an African-American and a man of God, provides the rights movement with insight and understanding that would be woefully lacking without him. Kenn is able to address issues that most of us simply can't, and he is able to educate us about the role of race in gun politics, while gently guiding us through the minefields of our own prejudices and preconceived notions.

I am blessed to call him friend and brother, and the rights movement is blessed to have him helping to lead the way.

Black Man with a Gun bridges a chasm, not only in the broader debate over freedom and firearms, but in the cultural perceptions of the players in that debate. It offers history and practical information in an easily accessible way and helps to draw us all closer together with greater understanding. I'm excited to see this revised edition of *Black Man with a Gun* being released. Not only will it help more people be safer and smarter about guns, it will help them to be more knowledgeable about the history and harm of the government-ordained crime known as gun control.

Jeff Knox, *The Firearms Coalition*

Published by White Feather Press. (www.whitefeatherpress. com)

ISBN 978-1-61808-087-5

Printed in the United States of America

Cover design created by Ron Bell of AdVision Design Group (www.advisiondesigngroup.com)

Publisher's note: Some of the names in this book have been changed to protect the privacy of the individuals involved.

White Feather Press

Reaffirming Faith in God, Family, and Country!

Acknowledgements

I bless God for my wife of 22 years. I also thank God for allowing me to see my son and daughter graduate college. I thank Him for using me to serve in the Gospel ministry and to pastor a church. I thank Him for the family and friends who have stuck by me and allowed me to be myself. I thank Him for grandparents and a mother who are young at heart. I thank Him for the gifts of creativity and compassion for others. I thank Him for allowing me to meet and befriend great men who have passed on. I thank Him for a faith that made me better as a human being. I thank Him for allowing me to be born an American and with the guts to keep it free.

I thank you for listening to my podcast, and the encouragement over the years. Thank you for buying this book and being a part of my community. I thank my peers from around the republic, from "sea to shining sea," who tirelessly fight to defend the right to keep and bear arms.

Dedication

This book is dedicated to my Christian wife, who is also the mother of the children that I am so proud of.

Contents

Introduction

When you first read or heard the term *Black Man With A Gun*, what was the first thing you thought of?

The response is different for many people but, believe it or not, this title was not created for shock value.

Whatever you thought might just reveal where you are in the gun-control debate.

The name was accidental. I didn't realize how it affected people. It was the title of my self-published book, *A Primer for New Gun Owners*. Nothing like it had been written in the African American community since Robert F. Williams wrote *Negroes with Guns* in 1962. I used the name also in 1999 because it was catchy for my website that advertised my services as a firearms instructor and grassroots activist.

I used it also to conceal the identity of my affiliation with the "They Who Must Not Be Named" federal agency who employed me, trained me and begrudgingly allowed me to "moonlight" as a firearms trainer as long as I didn't disclose the connection for my credentials. I am also a Marine Corps veteran, and a former federal police officer.

It has been my AKA ever since; and, because of it all, it has taught me a few things about life, people, gun control, America, politics, and the world.

You may never have heard of me, because I have worked in the background, and almost exclusively online, for two decades. I have been involved in almost every pro-rights event since 1991 that involved a person of color. I have lobbied the US Congress. I have testified in the state legislatures of Virginia, Texas, South Carolina, Michigan, Maryland, and Wisconsin. I have been in commercials for TV against racist gun laws, hundreds of radio talk show interviews, and have been featured in four documentaries.

I have worked with the National Rifle Association, Gun Owners of America, Second Amendment Foundation, American Sport Shooting Council and the CATO Institute, to name a few. I was a board member of the Law Enforcement Alliance of America. I have been the recipient of the National Rifle Association's *Carter-Knight Freedom Award*, the Citizens Committee for the Right to Keep and Bear Arms *Gun Defender Award of the Month*, and the *St. Gabriel Possenti Society's medal*.

This is an inside look at that journey, with lessons learned. You are about to get a candid look at everything you are not supposed to talk about in mixed company; i.e., sex, race, politics, religion, and now guns, from an ordained African-American Christian pastor who has worked almost thirty years in the Intelligence Community, protecting secrets and people while, at the same time, teaching both God and guns to a community afraid of and ignorant of its history.

I arrived here when I realized that the problem I was seeking to solve was bigger than I. I learned that scapegoating is a proven method of galvanizing the hearts and minds of a people. If you can effectively demonize an individual or a group, it's easier to rally for a cause against them.

In the absence of a "boogie man" or common enemy, I believe people will turn on themselves after a while. For some reason we need a purpose, a reason to circle the wagons. We need a dragon to slay.

The proof is in human history. There can be no appreciation of good without an evil. There has to be the girls against the boys, the old against the young, North v. South; or some form of an "us" v. "them".

"If you aren't with us, then you must be agin' us."

Winners and losers; Americans are hardwired like that. Good guys wear white hats. They get the girl at the end of the movie, kill the bad guy, and ride off into the sunset.

Today, in the real world, it is not politically correct to blame a group anymore. For example, it's no longer the Nazis, the Communists, and you can't blame the Negroes. African-Americans, trapped in self-pity, poverty, addictions, and a loss of hope, turn on each other. They can't effectively blame the white man, either, but allow many of the so-called talking heads to do so in absentia for street credibility.

The white man is blamed and assumed to be Republican even if he is not (as if one party can be faulted for all that is wrong in America). The white man was blamed for a while even by his own people as white women flexed their muscles and liberated themselves in spite of glass ceilings, sexism, and centuries of abuse. It is not often said, but quite often women press harder than necessary to assert their rightful position and become more like their oppressors and less like women.

This leads us to the mechanical device known as the gun as the socially acceptable object of our hate. We can use the images given to us by Hollywood to help us, because certain guns are used by all the bad guys in film. The images are easy to remember. Even if the illusions of what the firearms did are false, they are, nonetheless, effective.

For a politician, there are only a handful of evergreen topics. Gun control is one of them. A whole organization about it has existed since 1873. Understanding that, I have based the last two decades of my life as an iconic law-abiding figure of color on it.

The job was open, so I took it.

You are about to get to know a man who has almost been kicked out of two churches for his activism, lost promotions in the government, and almost lost his wife and family because he was caught up in the right to keep and bear arms.

Additionally, you'll learn about the history of gun control, the argument today, and the people involved from a guy who may well be the best who ever did it and got away with it.

I am the Black Man With A Gun® and this is my story, as well as the things I have learned on my journey.

.

CHAPTER I

__Grandma__

HAVE YOU EVER REMEMBERED DE-
tails about someone later in life that didn't mean
anything to you at the time? The first gun owner
I knew was my grandmother. I have mentioned her a few
times on my podcasts. I smile every time I hear of a woman
joining the firearms community. It doesn't matter if it is for
competition, to hunt, for self-defense, or to relieve stress.
My grandmother's shotgun saved my life.

Mary Goodman was the matriarch of many in her
Whaleyville, Virginia home near the Blackwater Swamp
Refuge area of Virginia. The town, near the border of North
Carolina, no longer exists. It was a place of refuge for many,
especially me. The mother of seven, grandmother of twenty-
three, and great-grandmother kept a loaded and unlocked
no-name shotgun behind the wood stove in the kitchen all
of my life. The shotgun was dark rusty brown from barrel to
butt stock.

Contrary to the hyperbole now told to the public, this shotgun was not used in the commission of a crime, and it didn't endanger any of the children who grew up with her. Grandma's house was the place where all old junk went for safe-keeping. There were old televisions, baby supplies, and furniture from every family. It was where you could get temporary stuff to supply your home. When you had your first child, there was a stroller or bassinet somewhere you could recycle. It was the place of refuge. When there was a family problem, kids and adults went there until they sorted things out.

Grandma's shotgun only moved away from behind the stove a few times that I can remember. It moved annually every New Year's Day, when she celebrated the Emancipation Proclamation at midnight. Then she fired it twice after hollering, "Happy New Year" into the dark, cold night. We laughed every year as she pruned the large pine tree next to the house with birdshot. A huge lichen-covered branch always came crashing down afterwards, adding to the sound.

I also noticed her gun had moved the night an angry, drunken stepfather came to take his family home. We didn't move that night, but he did. We heard the dialogue, heard my grandmother's southern diplomacy dripping with sweetness, backed up by the unknown fact that she had a shotgun on the other side of the screen door with her. I noticed the gun had moved when she was fixing us breakfast. I was one of the refugee kids who stayed there more than the other grandkids. There were three or four of us refugees there all the time. I stayed with her during every school break more than three days long from kindergarten to high school. It was like my second home. I didn't realize my mother sent me to stay with my grandmother for my own protection until recently. Domestic violence is a relatively accepted term today. I am a child survivor of it.

2

The shotgun moved once more when strange hunters crossed her one-acre property surrounded by Georgia-Pacific land we used. They were not the usual people with dogs and pick-up truck who would stop and chat with my grandparents, share venison and hunting news.

And the shotgun moved again when she shot a water moccasin that was coiled to strike me, near the grapevine, at the mouth of the swamp where I loved to play.

Grandmas' shotgun was like the sharpened ax that sat at the ready on the stump next to the pile of wood in the backyard of her home. We didn't touch either of them without asking my grandparents for permission. You can still teach responsibility, honor, love, and respect to your family. You don't need the government to do that for you. I am proof of this. I have done the same in my home with my children.

My grandmother is gone now, and the house has been destroyed by the relentless rigors of time, but the memories are still fresh. I appreciate all the women who seek to learn about firearms for themselves in spite of the lies from politicians, people with bodyguards, clergy, or organizations that want to preach banning everything as if we can't own a firearm responsibly and safely. Be wary of those who insult your intelligence, gender, or family in the name of child safety. My grandmother wasn't a scholar, but she made more sense than most of the people I meet today. The times might have changed, but people haven't.

I wouldn't be here if it weren't for an old black woman's love … and her gun.

CHAPTER 2

Black Hunters

I THOUGHT I HEARD A BLACK POWDER rifle go off yesterday behind my house, and it made me smile. It took me back to times with my grandmother. Hunting in America is still a timeless and beautiful tradition. The people who brave the weather conditions, enjoy the pursuit, and endure the time sitting motionless with a gun are representatives of what is good in our country. Almost all the hunters I know have a strong belief system and appreciation for life. There is a subset of hunters, however, that not much is known about. These are the Americans of African descent who hunt.

Believer or not, black people hunt. The African-American population comprises only 12.6 percent of the country; statistically, only 2 percent hunt. This may be a niche of a niche, but one that, if I follow the numbers, contains 778,586 people. To me, that is still a lot of potential for the shooting, outdoor, and trade show markets.

African-Americans have been hunting for food in the South since before the Civil War. It is more of a sport today. Before that, hunting was survival. Many men had to "poach" game to feed their families in a time when gun ownership was at worst illegal for a person of color, or they didn't own the land to hunt on. Today, it still comes down to land. One of the reasons for the lack of hunters of color is a land issue. Hunting is still a family thing. All the black hunters I know do so on privately owned land that has been in their families for generations.

Gun ownership for the black hunters of my childhood was not celebrated as much as it is today. The guns and rifles were like the axes and chainsaws they had. I remember seeing a half dozen squirrels, stripped of fur and stretched out in my aunt's kitchen sink soaking in brine. I remember that the smell of those squirrels smothered in gravy was enough to make a cardiologist wince. I remember hunters knocking on the screened porch, sharing parts of whitetail deer they had harvested that morning with my grandmother as they crossed her property. I remember wanting more venison than we had.

You ever wonder why there are so few African-Americans at your pro-gun events? For many shooters in the black community gun ownership makes them pariahs. They deal with gun bigotry, cultural alienation, and a lack of support. Let me illustrate one case with a guy named Phil and his family.

After Phil was married and became a father, protection of the house meant more to him than safeguarding property. He bought a shotgun. The shotgun was secured and forgotten until there was a home invasion down the street. Phil went back to the gun shop and bought his first handgun. He took all the steps required to legally own a handgun, which was more than he realized when he first had the thought. He did the paperwork, passed the national instant check, waited to be "Not Disapproved" by the Maryland State Police a week

5

later, and picked up his pistol ten days later. He took a class on concealed carry and learned that there was much he didn't know about the Second Amendment, the political games tied to the right to keep and bear arms, and now how his family and friends thought of him.

Buying a gun he intended to carry concealed, when and if he was approved to do so, alarmed his extended family. When he shared some of the things he'd learned about gun control with his brother-in-law, it started a big family fight. He was called a sell-out, an Uncle Tom, and blamed for the deaths of the drug dealers across town. They asked if he had joined the racist NRA. Phil was in shock at the responses. The more he talked about what he had learned, the more alienated he became. He did have one ally at the Sunday dinner. His cousin John, the family dissident and racist, (who blames everyone for his failures in life), was the only one who agreed he should have a firearm. His input didn't help Phil. Phil is like many Americans of African descent in the gun community ... alone and dejected.

Discrimination from your own family hurts. As new black gun owners, some find out that you have to defend the history of gun rights from slavery till the present, often with a hostile audience. While you are sharing facts, they are hitting you with every sound bite the anti-self-defense people have produced.

This happens because of conditioning over the past four hundred years. It is a lot like Stockholm syndrome. That is, a victim begins to express empathy toward his oppressor, sometimes to the point of defending him. After the Black Codes were instituted following the Civil War, black women lost husbands, and mothers lost sons, just for the act of carrying a firearm. To be found in possession of ammunition, or any parts of a weapon, could mean death by a mob. It was socially acceptable to summarily punish an armed black man. And that punishment ranged from public beatings, imprisonment, work camps, to torture/death. After a few centuries of that, every black woman who survived had it in her DNA to forbid bringing a sidearm into the house.

She doesn't care about the right to keep and bear arms argument. She just wants to save the lives of her children. This fear tactic is still being sold to mothers in the city. She doesn't believe gun ownership applies to her family. She doesn't have the luxury of philosophical debate about gun control. She just wants to save her race. It is hard to overcome that fear in the black home where the matriarch often rules and the facts are not there.

Phil's cousin told him to watch himself when he goes looking for training and to make sure he isn't used as a target, since he will be the only "colored" guy out there, as in the movie *Surviving the Game,* (1994), starring Ice-T, Rutger Hauer, and Gary Busey. So armed with all of that squirrely information, and with conflict in the back of Phil's mind, he decides to attend a pro-gun event.

You and I know that when Phil finally gets to a big gun event he will be welcomed warmly like everyone else. Unfortunately, he may not be culturally familiar with all the themes, things like big game hunting, NASCAR, and country music being prominent. While it may be American, it is not all of America.

This isn't every non-white male gun owner's story, just one with which I am familiar. I have spent the last twenty years mediating and encouraging people to understand that a gun is a tool, and personal accountability is what's important. You *know* that gun control is based on racist roots. You *know* that our country is still healing from it all. What you may not know is that all of us contribute to the success and failure of reaching new shooters of all colors, creeds, sexual preferences, and religions in America. We all just have to keep doing what's right even when no one is looking. It takes only one verbal mistake to set us back. One of the unwritten rules of becoming a gun owner is that you also have to become an ambassador for the cause. It's not a conservative, liberal, Republican, Democrat, black, or white thing. It's a rights thing.

> *"We must hang together, gentlemen...else, we shall most assuredly hang separately."*
>
> *– Benjamin Franklin*

CHAPTER 3

Superhero for My Son

I T HAD BEEN A LONG DAY ON THE RANGE with Ivy league graduates from around the world who soon would travel to unknown lands. My job at the Place That Shall Not Be Named was to train them to survive hostile environments, not to shoot themselves with the firearms they were issued, and to gain a little street smarts along the way. I scared a couple of them. Some didn't like me. I didn't laugh at their attempts to woo me. I didn't think they were cute, or as special as the government did. I knew that to them I was just an obstacle to overcome, a person they had to bear with for a few weeks. I was just a knuckle-dragger to them, just a step up from a caveman, with the knowledge of firearms.

It's okay; the feeling was mutual. I knew what I was, too. I was a great instructor, but I didn't belong there. I didn't have to be taught to survive in hostile environments, because

I had grown up in one. I didn't have a degree in political science, but I had a PhD from the school of hard knocks.

I had a son on the way, a new bride and daughter at home, and I had to provide. Maybe I could do this full time and teach people in the community how to protect themselves. Maybe I could help stop the accidents that occur because they have never been given adequate training about it when young kids find a gun in the home or on the playground. Maybe I could stop the violence if people understood the nature of the violence. It seemed like a good plan.

I don't know anything about business, but that is where I wanted to go. I wanted to become an entrepreneur and make a legacy for my son. I am not cut out for the politics of office work. I had already made enemies, and I hadn't even worked here long. Who would have thought being straightforward and honest would get you into hot water?

I failed some kid in the shooting house and found out his father was a director of some office. He is still going out to the field despite my recommendations. I just hope he doesn't kill someone on our side while he is out there.

Nobody had to tell me I was one of the first persons of color to be an instructor at this facility. I knew I was a mutant from the awkwardness of my peers. They weren't quite sure how to joke around me. I was used to it. I had been prepared for it since becoming a U.S. Marine. My first military occupation was that of a combat engineer and heavy equipment operator. It was a field that was coveted by longshoremen, construction workers, farmers, and bikers in the civilian world. I learned about country music, racism, chewing tobacco, rodeos, and more right there.

I probably threw these folks a curve by wearing a black cowboy hat out there instead of a baseball cap. There is nothing better to keep the elements and the stray brass from a friend shooting near you off of you.

As required, I asked for permission from my employers to moonlight as an instructor, and I got the evil eye. My request was approved with the restriction that I had to keep all my affiliation with the government a secret and couldn't share my extensive training, other than what I had gained from the Federal Law Enforcement Training Center and National Rifle Association. I didn't have the NRA training certificate, nor was I a member. I didn't know anything about them except they were deemed "political" by my outfit and had courses at a basic level we were all beyond.

The day my son was born was a pivotal moment for me. I wanted to be more than just his biological father. I wanted to be an action figure. That was a little of where the name Black Man With A Gun™ came from. It was someone apart from me. I wanted to become someone greater than myself.

I was not born on another planet, with abilities far greater than those of mortal men. I don't have super-powers given to me by birth, the sun, magic, or mutating DNA. I grew up in the sixties and enjoyed the "shoot-'em-up" movies – westerns, police dramas, and spy movies. In the midst of the civil rights struggle and low-income living, we got by. I was determined at a young age to do a couple of things. First, I wanted to see the world and, second, have a family. I wanted to be the best father in the world. The one other folks' kids wanted to hang around. I wanted to be knowledgeable and accessible, cool and wise, in great shape and able to play with my kids as long as they were kids. I wanted to be everything a father was supposed to be. There was no book on fatherhood. There were no examples to emulate. Of all the friends I had, few had fathers they bragged about. I was determined to be different for my kids, even if it took superhuman effort.

I was told my natural father was my "uncle" until my grandmother's Freudian slip told me different. Daddy was the hardest-working man I ever saw. He had two jobs and half a dozen side projects that brought in money from time to time. Both of my "fathers" lived and partied hard. I was determined to not be like either of them with my child when it was born. I had lived in a world of fantasy as a kid. It was safer there than in the real world. My "stepfather" and mother fought like prizefighters, and furniture got moved out of place. In my mind I escaped to a happier place. It was a place of honor, valor. and heroics. The bad guys were really evil, and gray was just a shadow or the background.

My love of watching westerns, police dramas, and spy movies seemingly influenced my life, as I enlisted in the U.S. Marine Corps right out of high school. Later I became an employee of the federal government. I did a host of different things while inside, ranging from physical security to world-changing operational stuff. It was through my travels, exploits, and failures that I realized the life I was living was not conducive to longevity, or to any of the dreams I'd had as a child.

It was late October, and my wife was a week late for giving birth. I was having second thoughts about the whole thing and wondered if I was even capable of being the type of man necessary to raise a child and be a good husband. In my mind, I was a product of survival, not proper upbringing. I had survived domestic violence, civil wars, bombings, terrorist attacks, and international politics. I was a good government employee, but a rogue warrior. I was good at my job and loyal to nothing except my country and God. It is the latter that I learned must be instilled into every heart if there is to be any humanity left after the world takes a bite out of your soul. To me, I was not father material despite how much I wanted to be. I had fidelity issues. I was afraid. How could I be successful as a parent when there were no templates, no examples, and no guidance to follow? Any man with a penis can be a father, but it takes someone special to be a daddy. I come from a long line of absentee fathers.

Each child deserves a chance not just to survive but to thrive. More often than not, we as parents fail to do all we can do personally for our children. We parent by proxy. Love is sacrificial. We hope that some coach, teacher, clergy, or someone will do what we are not sure of doing. And as a result, we fail.

The day he was born was one of the warmest Novembers I could remember. I was tired of waiting for my baby to be born and finally told my wife to just page me when the contractions were coming. I figured by the time I got there from the secret base where I was training federal agents how to shoot, I would have cut down the wait time. A lot of thoughts were going on in my mind. I always wanted to be a great father, a daddy. Better than Cliff Huxstable (*The Cosby Show*), better than Mr. Cunningham (*Happy Days*), better than Mr. Cleaver (*Leave it to Beaver*), but I didn't see it. Like Popeye, "I yam what I yam." Nine months ago, this hadn't seemed so bad. I had just gotten married to my trusted friend. That alone was scary enough.

Now I was becoming a parent. Damn! No instruction manual. I can't blow up, shoot down, or incinerate my fears. I had overcome IRA bombs, the Taliban, Communist rebels in different continents, but this was freaking me out. Luckily the ride home to civilization was long.

No page, no phone calls. The baby hadn't arrived yet, and the munchkin was two weeks late. I guess he didn't want to be born on Halloween, and I don't blame him. The house was dark when I pulled up in the driveway. It was close to eleven p.m., and I dropped my sidearm back in the safe, emptied my pockets, (there was also extra ammo in there somewhere), dropped the clothes in the hamper, and headed for the hot shower. Man, that was looking good right about now. The steam cleared my head and washed the smell of cordite and a week's worth of swamp dirt off me. I decided I'd better check my boots before the Mrs. woke up. Knowing me, I had tracked dirt all the way in. The girl is cleaner than the drill instructors I used to have. The blue light from the television illuminated the bedroom, and I easily crawled into bed next to the mother of my soon to be born son. Aaaaah. A bed can feel orgasmic when you have been away from home for a while. Sleep came fast, but two hours later I woke up to the phrase, "I think my water just broke." I think I went into hyperspace, because I got the Mrs. up and out in no time. We got to the hospital really fast, because at two a.m. there isn't much traffic. Hospitals are funny about baby deliveries. They don't really care. What was a significant emotional event, something I teach, is routine to them. We got settled in a pod, and I stood there holding my wife's hand until the sun rose, as the monitors beeped and recorded the rhythms of my son making his approach into the world. I felt like a horse and started to lose it when some little dwarf doctor with an anesthesia cart came in and asked my wife if she wanted an epidural. (That is when they administer anesthesia through a needle in the woman's spine to make her more comfortable during childbirth.) I was asked to leave and was glad to comply. My knees were killing me. I was asleep on my feet like a horse, feeling like I was standing watch in a triage unit. Hospitals are interesting places. They are a city all their own. The coffee shop was the meeting place for couples, watchmen, and people like me who had been on duty with family. The coffee was like mud, but it went down like premium stuff because I needed it. By the time I got back upstairs, the Mrs. was a different person. She was obviously feeling no pain and happier than when I had brought her into this joint six hours ago. On the other side of the curtain, a man was screaming at the mother of his soon-to-be-born child to the point where I thought he needed an attitude adjustment. I was a little cranky, and beating down a probable wife-beater might have cheered me up. The Mrs. saw my face and reached for my arm.

I was about to be a father in a few minutes, I could tell. And the fear came back. My family tree is a shrub. My father was raised by his mother, and he basically hated his father. I had found out who my father was at the age of nine; and though I thought he was the coolest brother on the planet, we weren't close. I saw him maybe once a year. How do you stop a generational curse? How do you do the right thing when your DNA says run? Before I could contemplate the universe, some mechanical monitor started to sound. Curtains flew open and a gang of pale-green-pajama-wearing people and a few big ladies in multicolored cotton outfits pushed me out of the way and snatched the Mrs. (So much for natural childbirth and all the time suffering through Lamaze class as the only husband in the joint.) Something was wrong, and the little ninja was in trouble. I was left standing there like a late mechanic on a NASCAR pit crew. Oh well, nothing left to do but sit down. Didn't even know there was a television in the room till then. I found a remote and clicked on the TV. The probable wife-beater on the other side of the curtain had left; his wife was obviously battered, at least emotionally, and this kid was in for a hell I knew too well.

The chair in the corner of the room felt good again. The television droned on with the morning news. My eyelids began to close as I remembered how I got here. As sleep overcame me, I dreamed. *The difference between a father and a daddy is love. Love conquers a multitude of sins. No greater love does a man have than to lay his life down for a friend. And though I speak many languages but don't have love, I am just making noise. If I have the gift of prophecy and am super smart, and believe in God but not real love, I am nothing. Durn, where is this coming from? Love is sacrifice. Your wife is in trouble.* That last thought snapped me awake. I got up and walked down the hall toward the delivery room. A nurse said that they were performing an emergency "C-section" on my wife, and they would call me when I could come in. That didn't sound good. I returned to my chair in the corner of the little room I had been sitting in. I dozed again but was awaked by the sound of a loudspeaker right next to my ear. "MR. BLANCHARD, YOUR SON IS IN THE HALLWAY!"

I looked up at the bright light reflecting the sunrise off the opposite side of the building into this wing of the hospital and mumbled aloud, "What is he doing in the hallway? My son? I have a son! Oh!"

I jumped up and looked down the hall at a small Filipino nurse carrying what looked like a yardstick covered in baby blankets. Either the kid was long or the lady was short. My eyes betrayed me, and I couldn't focus as well as I wanted to.

"Mr. Blanchard?"

"Yes."

"This is your son."

She tried to hand him to me, but I wouldn't take him. I didn't know how to hold a baby, not a new one, not one fresh out of the oven. He was obviously delicate, pure, innocent, breathing his first breaths of air under a cocoon of clean, sterilized cotton.

"Mr. Blanchard, please take your son."

"No ma'am. You just take him to where he has to go."

"Don't you want to hold him?"

"Yeah, but I don't want to do something wrong."

We played this game for a few minutes, where she offered up the bundle but I wouldn't extend my arms out to take it, as we walked into a nursery with a hundred other new people. She finally gave up and placed him in a see-through bed and opened the blanket, revealing a funny-looking little child wearing a sky blue beanie. He had light-colored eyes and a miniature version of my facial features.

"What is his name?"

I don't know if it was sleep deprivation, fatigue, or a spiritual block, but the grandiose name the Mrs. had talked about for nine months escaped the Read Access Memory of my brain.

"His name is Kenneth, like his father."

"Oh he is a junior then?"

"No, he'll be the second."

There was a joke in my family that I had just fallen into. I am a country boy at heart and my family comes from the rural south. We have probably ten juniors in my family. The nurse left me alone with the little blue-hat-wearing Smurf who stared at me with all the focus of a U.S. Marine awaiting orders.

"Hey, little dude. I guess you know I am your father. When I was born my father wasn't with me. When he was born his father wasn't with him. I am not a good man. Haven't been the best husband to your mother, but because of you I am going to try to be. I don't know how to change your diapers or do all the right stuff where you are concerned, but I am going to try. I don't know what is going to happen tomorrow, or where you are going to end up, but I am going to make sure you get the best I can provide of my time, my attention. I am going to love you, little dude, unconditionally. You got some rough genes in you. You have some tough genes in you. The

17

Bible says something about never leaving you nor forsaking you. That's my promise to you. Today, I stop a generational curse. You will be the first Blanchard male in my family that knows who, what, and where his father is. Deal?"

A little hand reached up out his blanket and I extended my pinky finger to him. He grabbed a hold of it and held it a long time. The contract was sealed and a daddy was born. Many challenges came afterward. Most of them were internal. I had to choose between pleasing myself temporarily and working to rebuild a home I'd almost destroyed. It required more energy than I thought. To deny yourself and put others first sounds easier than it is. You get no reward for doing the right thing. You get no pat on the back from your boys.

Baby seats don't work on a motorcycle. A child seat doesn't look cool in a Corvette.

I have learned it takes six weeks to change a habit or way of life. Each step is wrought with temptations to quit and go back to what you know. Love is sacrifice. It's not all romantic music and warm, fuzzy feelings. Sacrifice sucks. Sometimes you have to give up, give in, and change. It is not for the weak. It takes super-human effort to deny yourself. It takes power you are not born with to not call the honey that dropped a phone number in your lap. It takes a faith not preached on television.

In the movies, superheroes often have personal issues that folks seem to overlook. Batman was warped by revenge. Superman was an illegal alien. All the X-Men have birth defects to overcome. Bruce Banner has an anger management issue. Spiderman has a problem with self-esteem. Any man who honors his marriage vows and loves his wife as he loves himself is operating under the "supernatural." The man who spends quality time with his child to teach and inspire is far superior to other mere mortals. Narcissism, infidelity, and immaturity plague the planet. Being strong enough to lead a household is not taught, respected, nor seen often. Being mature enough to withstand the trend to seek pleasure by any means necessary and instead to seek the best for your baby can be as tough as bending steel with your bare hands. It's easier to get laid than to get a sandwich. Show me a brother with the courage to braid his daughter's hair, and I'll show you tough. Show me a man who will willingly shop for her clothes, and I'll show you strength. Show me a man who will lead by example with his wife until that woman trusts and esteems him, and I'll show you a real man.

It's currently cool to look effeminate, act like a buffoon, or portray yourself as a pimp. All three of these characteristics support a weak man. Clowns belong in a circus, not in a family. Pimps, by definition, prostitute and take advantage of others. In the animal kingdom, mosquitoes, maggots, leeches, and other life-draining organisms fit into this category, too. One of the many differences between an animal and a man is that a man can learn from the mistakes of others. Too many of us prefer to be beasts instead of men. Sometimes you have to ask yourself why that is.

Real strength is developing into the man you were born to be. Since we are not immortal, you have a limited amount of time to achieve personal success and make an impact on the world before you leave out of here. Each of us was born with a gift or a talent that is unique to us. That is why you were born. Too many of us go to our graves with that unachieved gift lying within us. There are no biological accidents. I don't care what you have been told or believe. A man unsure of his purpose has no focus and no real power. A shotgun has a large blast and can be quite destructive, but the impact it can make doesn't go very far. A laser beam, on the other hand, is a focused beam of energy that can cut through steel, carry information and sound, and travel at the speed of light across miles. I was trying to figure out what my focus was going to be.

When I was a kid, my father's generation believed that as long as a man provided financially for his family he was fulfilling his duty as a father and husband. We now know that money is never enough. Your circumstances can hinder you, but they don't have to stop you. I realized that all superheroes had a problem. I had a lot going on when I determined to visit the National Rifle Association for the first time. I decided it was time to press on.

CHAPTER 4

First Shot

THE **N**ATIONAL **R**IFLE **A**SSOCIATION (NRA) was the pop standard for what the public accepted in regard to training, so I thought I'd at least check them out. I found out how prejudiced I was when I crashed an NRA board meeting in Arlington, Virginia one day. I figured I'd sneak into the place and observe some good ol' boys and find one who wanted to talk about the NRA and give me some inside information. I walked into the ballroom wearing my regular blue jeans, black leather Harley Davidson jacket, and cowboy boots (who was the redneck, right?) – into a room full of tuxedos and after-six wear. The members of the board were politicians, business-men, CEOs of companies, and members of academia. I was a little embarrassed and obviously not dressed for this event. I was heading to the door, (as the only other African Americans I saw in the room except for one college profes-sor from Rutgers University were on the wait-staff), when two directors stopped me. For the next couple of minutes I got what I wanted plus some. Both welcomed me to the event but warned me to stay clear of the media who were present. They said the media would use me in a negative fashion to portray me as a "bubba" gun owner. My nickname was Bubba, (before Forrest Gump), so I was intrigued.

They began telling about the need for more people of color on the board and in the fight for gun rights. They messed up; they created a monster. These two old guys gave me more black history than I had ever heard. One of the directors was from Michigan and told me about Dr. Ossian Sweet. I had never heard that story before. The other introduced me to the Deacons of Defense, a group that was started during the Civil Rights era. (Again, a name I had never heard.) I work around professional liars every day. I knew truth when I heard it, but I was still going to verify it. I left after an hour, with my head spinning from all that I had seen and heard. I was invited to attend a dinner two weeks later and became a member of the Law Enforcement Alliance of America soon afterwards.

I changed my duties at work so I could work the midnight shift to be home with my son during most of the day. Working midnights, after my shift and on my way home, I often stopped in to a local radio station to sit in with my mentor and friend, Bernie McCain. Bernie amazed me. He was a sage and a wealth of information. Bernie confirmed what the NRA guys had told me and added to my insatiable appetite for history and knowledge.

When I went to the gun store to offer my services, I was ignored. It was not from the storeowners but from the people I was looking to as future customers. I got my first dose of reality about the culture and conditioning of African-American people and the gun issue. I didn't realize I looked too young to know anything. I couldn't tell anyone I was trained by the best in the world. When I passed my business cards out in public I was berated for promoting violence in the black community. I had no idea that what I was trying to do would not be accepted in my own community. I got verbally abused a lot by people who look like me. I understood why Harriet Tubman, the black Moses of the Underground Railroad, had to pull her gun on slaves sometimes to get them to leave the plantation or not run back to it once freed. Slavery really messes with your head. It is a generational curse. I pressed on.

When I arrived at the Safari International-hosted dinner as a guest of several of the new friends I'd met at the NRA directors' meeting, I had new business cards. I was now the CEO of African American Arms and Instruction, Inc. (A3i) I was going to be the black Moses for gun rights. I still am. In the next eight years I taught, organized a gun club, was interviewed, and wrote for a number of print media that have come and gone. I learned that grassroots doesn't make any money unless you are a nonprofit. I didn't have the chutzpah or knowledge to make that happen. I struggled. I learned. I experimented. I learned a lot about human nature, politics, sociology, and anthropology, all while still working for the US government, doing a number of things, sometimes historical, always unable to disclose, always in controversy. I lived two lives and became two people.

I got into the pro-rights movement by accident. I just wanted to take what the government had taught me and help the people in my community live safer through training. I didn't want to be in politics. I didn't understand how political gun ownership is. I didn't know that people of color, specifically Americans of African descent in most cities that I was trying to help, were discombobulated about guns. It was the swimming pool all over again.

When I was in basic training at Parris Island, SC to become a U.S. Marine, all recruits had to get classified to what level they could swim or operate in the water. It was the largest indoor pool I had ever seen. It had been a rough week for me, and I couldn't do anything right, I thought. I was so glad when they told us to put on swimming trunks and jump in the water. I knew it would be one of the few places the Drill Instructors couldn't get me for a few minutes. I love water. Like going to the chapel, this was going to be a peace break.

Well, over a hundred young men jumped into the pool. That was quite a sound. I swam to the deeper end and floated effortlessly for several minutes as I noticed that the room was growing quieter. Underneath me, I saw men in scuba gear patrolling like reef sharks. When I finally looked to the wall where we had all launched, I noticed that there were at least seventy black men, dripping water and shaking from the experience. I looked around and wondered, *Did I miss the whistle*? I tried to whisper to my bunkmate, who was also out of the water, "Why are you out of the water?" He cautiously whispered back, "The brothers don't swim." I thought to myself, "Damn, what am I, a mutant?"

Well, here I was, a certified law enforcement firearms trainer, with citations from the Federal Law Enforcement Training center and the NRA for expert shooting. I was not the only black man with a gun. My grandmother was a heckuva shot with her no-name, rusty, dusty, single-barreled shotgun.

I also knew I wasn't the only U.S. military veteran, person with a security or law enforcement background, socially conscious person that owned a gun, either. They were college educated and traditionally trained by the hunters in their homes, people who looked like me. Every relative I have in Virginia as old as my mother has a modern musket of some type. It was as important as a lantern. It was another tool.

You've probably heard the statistics about crime in the "urban" environment, right? Someone has promised you that if you vote for them they are going to solve all your problems. Someone was lying to somebody. We do have a crime and violence problem in our cities, but it's not the fault of the gun owner. Lying is popular when it comes to firearms. It's almost like fishing. The fish I caught was this big!

Why is crime so bad in the city? I can give you a few reasons: overcrowding, poverty, addictions, ignorance, unemployment, and hopelessness. It doesn't matter what color you are if you are stuck. If you choose to live in closer proximity to others than you would in a rural environment, you give up space and personal freedom to get along.

Additionally, almost everything said about guns always has a racist "black" spin to it. You might not notice it now because you are used to it; but because I am so immersed in the roots of this issue, I know. What color is an assault weapon? Did you guess black? Believe it or not, people who like modern sporting rifles even call them black guns. They are, in effect, modern muskets.

Gun buybacks are big media events which happen in predominantly "black" churches, with black ministers allowing it to be done in the sanctuary. If the people were in it for some propaganda, ignorance, or fear, that wouldn't be tolerated. Gun "buyback" programs are misnamed. You cannot buy back something you didn't own in the first place. What it is really is a way for rich people to get a tax deduction, and for an inner city church to get some press. Criminals don't turn in guns except to get rid of evidence. Gun owners know guns are worth more than a gift card or tennis shoes. And if you have actually been to a gun buyback, you've seen stuff that (1) is inoperable, (2) will probably never make it to get destroyed, if of value or (3) hardly anything turned in. Why would anyone support the turn-in of legal property simply to destroy it, when it can be sold to law-abiding individuals at a profit?

And the biggest lie is that black people don't hunt, collect, own, compete with, or want to own a firearm to protect themselves. If you agree with that, are you saying people of color are less responsible? How about the thought that only white people, rednecks, and other nasty-named people own guns? If you hear a lie long enough you will start to believe it. And this is one of the ways black people get the facts twisted.

I was balancing the dream of entrepreneurism, maturity, a new marriage, fatherhood, a career that was in trouble because of poor financial decisions, and jobs that didn't mix.

When I started working at Mount Sinai Baptist Church in NW Washington, DC I was on the comeback trail. I had survived a cat and mouse game overseas protecting a diplomat and his family from terrorist assassins. I had survived the celebratory partying that goes along with the job after you don't get killed at the end of the day, week, and month. I had survived persecution and the results of my own issues working in the federal government. My managers hated that I was moonlighting as a firearms trainer and gun rights activist. They watched for anything I did that could be construed to be against policy, the law, or national security. Every time I appeared on camera, or my name appeared in print, I was scrutinized. I had promotions withheld. I would always lose the next assignment by a few minute "points" to some pinhead who lived near the boss or played the game better. I was a GS-10 for ten years. While that won't mean much to you if you are retired from the government already, it does if you are currently inside. I struggled with my business. I was trying to get the gun business I had started to pay for itself. It wasn't.

I am a risk-taker. It has served me well. It has kept me alive. Financially, it is not a good thing. In a way, I gambled with the family finances. I lost. I learned there is a bigger business to sucker optimistic entrepreneurs out of any money they make. Everything from expensive business cards, websites, legal advice, and credit you don't need until you are making over 10K is unnecessary. I can show you ninety-nine things that don't work.

CHAPTER 5

Pistol-Packing Preacher

BROKE, BUT STILL WORKING, MY marriage hanging on by a thread only God could see, winding down from a high-adrenaline occupation, I applied for a job as a sextant at this church. It was a good place to be. I was broke financially and spiritually. I could use the extra money and I needed to be closer to God. It was an excuse to be there more than once a week and more than three times a year. I spent the evenings cleaning and opening doors for the many activities that happened Monday through Friday at the church. I saw the best and the worst of many. I saw how people treat others when it is not Sunday. I watched people belittle and snub the less fortunate. I smiled as they tried to "punk" me not knowing my background. Two things happened there every evening: I wrote for a few minutes every afternoon on the first edition of this book, and before I left at night I talked to God in the sanctuary, absent all the foolishness, personalities, and rituals. God healed me.

I resigned from the position after a year and received The Call into the gospel ministry. Some at the church were happy, and some were not. Those who were not were the same ones I had seen mistreat people, and they didn't like the fact that I might have the ear of the pastor or be sitting in a higher place in the church than they were. They were right and looked for opportunities to bring me down. Out of the twenty or so ministers on the rostrum, I became the pastor's aide and his Armor Bearer. I took it to be like his protector and confidant. I was hardwired to do that anyway. When my first book was published it was bittersweet. I had to leave a lot of details out that I have shared here. I paid to have it edited and didn't get what I wanted. I was indebted to my cousin the football star, and that worried me. It is true that you don't want to borrow money from relatives. I love him. I am proud of him. But we have gone through some stuff. To market the book, I had a website created that started my journey on the World Wide Web. The URL *blackmanwithagun* was born, and I proudly had it put on the back of my pick-up truck in reflective white lettering. Yes, I did! It made the deacons cringe. Police officers waved in support. Gun people beeped their horns, and everyone else kept their hands "ten and two" on the steering wheel and avoided eye contact as they passed. It was good times.

When my picture appeared in *The Washington Times* and the *Washington Business Journal*, there was talk in the church of taking away my license to preach. The pastor defended me and nothing was said to me openly.

Ten days before the terrorist attacks on September 11, I gave my trial sermon on the first Psalm to a small crowd at my home church. I was a new minister, a new author, and trying to find my way as a pistol-packing preacher. I saw both the praise that came from being a published author and the disapproval for being pro-gun. I saw the hypocrisy and the elitism for the first time in my own race. The Holy Bible was used as the reason, but through study I found that the argument was weak.

Religion and the Bible are often used in arguments against people's, especially African Americans', owning firearms. Before we start to question Christianity as it relates to self-defense, let me remind you how Africans became Christians. Religion has been used to manipulate black people since our arrival in this country.

Religion has always been important in the African society. Before we were brought to this country, religion was a daily, minute-to-minute concern, not something relegated to a special, once-a-week occasion. While the transition from old beliefs to modern day religious practices was not done overnight, the conviction about the importance of religion was never lost.

After realizing slaves could be converted to Christianity, Quakers and other religious groups in the 19th century began a crusade. Some of the churches, like the Methodists and the Baptists, began to send ministers among the slaves to convert them. The emotionalism and the evangelism of the Methodist and Baptist Churches appealed to the slaves much more than any of the other denominations. On the poorer plantations the lower-class whites were also more apt to be Baptist or Methodist than Episcopal or Presbyterian. If the Catholic Church had canvassed the South like the other churches of that time, most of the African community today would be Catholic.

Since the church holds a special place in our heritage as black Americans, it is also where we are attacked political-ly. Proof of this is demonstrated daily whenever a political leader is trying to obtain an office or gain support. Today gun buybacks or gun turn-ins are the order of the day.

A look back at history reminds US that some of the be-liefs about which we are so emotionally concerned are based upon facts we don't really know. Christianity and religion in general are no exceptions. The uninformed and easily duped might think the Bible is opposed to self-defense; but if you look to the Bible for reference and guidance regarding this issue, you'll find that Judeo-Christian tradition is non-paci-fistic. Exodus 22:2, for example, allows for the killing of a night-time burglar.

The Old Testament has several other similar examples, like the one in Genesis 14:14, where Abraham formed a posse in order to rescue his nephew Lot from kidnappers. So what about the New Testament? I'd argue that, though Jesus changed the Law of Moses from an "eye for an eye" into one that forgives all for "those who trespass against us," He also allowed His disciples to arm themselves with swords as they went on their missionary journeys. If the disciples had the right to defend themselves while on the job for Christ, so does the businesswoman who is on her way to church at night.

While the Christian, as a member of God's Kingdom, is supposed to forgive his or her enemies and persecutors, it doesn't say anywhere in the Bible that bearing arms in self-defense is wrong. What it does say, in many different ways, is that you will be accountable for your actions, whatever you do.

My definition of *religion* is man's preferences for the worship of God. As humans we impose, enforce and sub-scribe to a lot of stuff that is not of God.

Gun prohibitionists who look to the Bible for support do not cite specific interdictions of weapons, because there are none. Instead they point to general passages about peace and love as the basis for their stance. None of the references used is in context to a threat to a person's life. *"Do not resist an evil person. If someone strikes you on the right cheek, turn to him the other also" (Matthew 5: 38-39)* is a blow to pride, but not a threat to life. *"Love your enemies and pray for those who persecute you" (Matthew 5: 43)* is right on, but, again, it does not equate to a lethal force encounter.

One of the most controversial, misunderstood and maligned issues in the African-American and Jewish communities is guns. One of the reasons is that in these two cultures, religion is connected to our ethos. It is who we are as a people. We cannot turn it off, and it is used against US in the same fashion.

Since birth I have been a defender or a protector of some type. When I became a minister, it was assumed that I would change and become more like my peers. I rejected it. I am not like my peers. I did not come up the same way they did in the church. My testimony is different. I emulate no one but Jesus. I reject the notion that Christians are not spiritual or lack faith if they choose to arm themselves to protect themselves. But that line of thinking is not accepted in the traditional black church.

Does anyone really believe persons of faith should allow themselves or their families to be maimed or killed by a criminal? What confuses most Christians is the Sixth Commandment. Too many times it has been interpreted as *"Thou shall not kill;"* however, the original translation was *"Thou shall not murder,"* meaning the premeditated execution of killing another human being, which was first mentioned in Genesis, when Cain murdered his brother Abel (Genesis 4:8).

I have been asked on occasion how I can justify carrying a gun and being a Christian at the same time. This is always posed by someone who is trying to trip me up. It can either be a devout Christian asking the question or a hedonistic heathen; it doesn't matter. There are those who believe, or choose to believe, that a Christian must be absolutely passive in all things. I am not just referring to those Christians who ride a horse and buggy. Christians of most every denomination have asked me about my views on self-defense. Some are genuinely seeking an answer. Others just want to chastise me for not being as "faithful" as they are.

Many will accept every modern worldly convenience but scoff at the idea of trying to protect oneself or the life of another. Their attitude seems to be that "God will protect us." They do have a valid point. God will protect us from the evils of this world, if He so chooses. I would rather have God on my side than a battery of Sidewinder missiles. Indeed, our God can protect us. However, that attitude would lead one to believe that he could walk through Harlem wearing a Ku Klux Klan outfit, campaigning for George Wallace, and "God will protect us." God could get you through that, but Jesus said we should not tempt God. I tend to agree with His assessment.

Choosing to carry a firearm for self-defense is not a murderous act. "Gun" does not equal "murder." My answer to how I can be a Christian and carry a gun at the same time is based on my understanding that a Christian is a follower/disciple of Jesus the Christ. There are those who believe, or choose to believe, that a Christian must be absolutely passive in all things. Christ never said or claimed to be a pacifist. A pacifist chooses not to partake in war or violence no matter what. There are times when a living being must defend itself. Even lambs have teeth.

Contrary to popular belief, Christians are not unspiritual or lacking faith in choosing to arm themselves to protect themselves in addition to praying for protection. Does anyone really believe a person of faith should allow himself or his family to be maimed or killed by a criminal?

Murder was, and still is, of course, wrong; however the Bible does permit justifiable homicide. This is clearly shown in Genesis 9,

> *"Whoever sheds the blood of man, by man shall*
> *his blood be shed, for in the image of God has*
> *God made man."*

Although a different argument, did you know that the Old Testament of the Bible also allows for capital punishment?

"You shall forfeit the life of anyone guilty of slaying the innocent."

The Bible also has clear guidelines on using force when an intruder breaks into the home:

> *"If he is caught breaking in and struck so that*
> *he dies, the defender is not guilty of bloodshed,*
> *but if it happens after sunrise, he is guilty of*
> *bloodshed." (Exodus 2:2).*

The logic in this is still valid. At night it is harder to recognize the threat, and the household is more in danger at night that in the daytime. Anyone who would break into your home while you are there is not nice.

The Bible also clearly allows for people to arm themselves to overcome and deter attackers. In fact, priests in the Old Testament gave blessings to warfare, not condemning warriors (Joshua 6:2(1); Jesus was even in support of his disciples' protecting themselves when collecting money for the group,

> *"But now, if you have a purse take it, and also*
> *a bag, and if you don't have a sword, sell your*
> *cloak and buy one."*

The disciples said,

*"See, Lord, here are two swords." "That is
enough," He replied. (Luke: 2:2).*

Jesus changes the heart, not necessarily the occupation.
I learned this while learning what my role was to be as a
minister. It was a tough lesson. When He called men to follow Him, He never said they had to put down their swords to
be called disciples. Simon Peter, one of, if not the closest of,
friends to Jesus, carried a weapon. Jesus knew it. He knew in
advance what Peter would do if attacked. I advocate personal
responsibility and accountability.

Both the Old and New Testaments teach individual self-
defense, even if it means taking the assailant's life in certain
circumstances.

Our country was founded on Christian principles, but
technically it is not a Christian nation. Our system respects
the belief systems of others. And at the expense of being politically correct, we are becoming morally bankrupt. We have
yet to live out the true meaning of our creed, which placed
humanity under a higher standard, the Deity, thus making all
men equal under God.

We are so free today, though, that we want to give away
our freedom for the semblance of safety. I have learned that
we need faith. We are born looking for something or someone to believe in. When something tells you not to jump
off the bridge, or something keeps you from making a bad
decision, I call that something God. I understand that some
people have a hard time believing in God. Their disbelief
is reinforced by the acts of clergy, churches, scientific theo-
rems, and the quotations of respected men.

Faith, however, is a power source that is not reliant upon
gender, doctrine of men, or fashion. When you boil up all the
mumbo-jumbo, all the things you don't understand, faith is

really a matter of choice. I choose to believe in God, not as a crutch but as a source of power.

In the cases where the disciples wanted to fight, it was because of their desire to force the hand of God. They didn't understand the need for the sacrifice of Christ for the remission of sins. They didn't understand His mission. All of His answers were related to that context. It is the context of His statements that is so misused today.

Even Judas Iscariot, the zealot, the much-maligned disciple, was a trusted treasurer. Judas was secretly involved in the overthrow of the government before joining Christ. He thought after he witnessed the power of Jesus that if he could get folks to capture Him, Jesus would call down a legion of angels to wipe out oppressive Rome and the puppet governments. He had no clue that Jesus would lay down His life after being seized.

No sane individual would hesitate to defend himself from a rabid dog or a poisonous snake, but are the two-legged vipers of this world any better than animals? An animal does that which comes naturally to him. Children of Satan do that which comes naturally to them: being evil.

Can God protect us from those who would do us harm? Absolutely. However, just as He has given us brakes on our cars to save us from crashing, He has also given to us the tools necessary to defend ourselves. As Christian men, God not only allows us to protect our families, but He also expects us to protect those whom He has placed in our care. It's a stewardship thing. This may seem contrary to the mandate for us to "turn the other cheek," but again, it has to be in context. In that case, for example, it had to do with which hand would be used to strike a person and the Aramaic culture of the time. It also demonstrated the great strength and character of Christ, to turn the other cheek as Jesus intended.

That is not a commandment to be weak. Jesus never operated from a position of weakness. In fact, nothing ever happened to Him that He did not allow. He was the strongest man the world has ever seen. Christianity is not for wimps.

We have it twisted that being a follower of Jesus should make you a doormat.

There is a time for everything. *A time for peace and a time for war...*

I have seen what man is like with the absence of faith. Personally, I am a Christian by conversion. I worship in the style of a Baptist as a choice. It is not the only way; it is just what I am comfortable with. The Way is so simple we blow it.

Faith is real. Faith has power. It is a power given by belief in God. We believe so many things smaller than God, but we stutter when we talk about religion. We falter when someone asks us what we believe.

What do you believe? We are free to believe just about anything, and that gets us into trouble. Freedom is like that, but I would have it no other way.

The absence of law, rules, and social order sounds good, but it is not a place you want to live in for a long time. People by design need to feel a sense of belonging and acceptance, whether it comes from a large social group or from clubs, groups, organizations, teams, gangs, or tribal connections. Someone wrote that we are born with a need to be loved and never outgrow it. We need to love and be loved (sexually and non-sexually) by others. In the absence of these elements, many people become susceptible to mental issues that start out as loneliness, anxiety, and clinical depression. This need for belonging can often overcome the physiological and security needs, depending on the strength of the peer pressure for a feeling of control and belonging.

I know some think we can do great without anyone, but that is only because we haven't had the misfortune to test that theory. Think about the punishment we give prisoners: solitary confinement. Being left alone to our own thoughts can be brutal.

Faith also gives you a foundation for peace. The absence of faith says that whatever is legal goes. Whatever is trendy goes. Whatever we say is right today wins. You can do many things legally that are not morally, ethically, or socially right. While that sounds nice, I found out that I could jump higher with a platform. We need a base. We all do better with a compass. My platform is *the Gospel*. If it didn't work I wouldn't defend it, but it does.

In ancient China, Shaolin Monks (another religion) perfected the art and science of fighting to protect the weak. It still takes someone with a higher moral code than self-preservation to go into harm's way for another. I look at gun owners today like this. It is this belief that keeps me in the gun culture. I have discovered that the people who carry firearms legally and consequently submit to all the overreaching requirements to do so have such character.

The Shaolin believed that only the noble men (Monks) of high morals were to be taught the true combat arts. On no account should a bad man who didn't follow true "Tao" (the way) be taught.

Followers of Jesus Christ were called members of "The Way."

> *"I am the way and the truth and the life. No one comes to the Father except through me."*
> *John 14:6*

Like many things over time, men have perverted or used different things for personal gain. I seek to remind others about the need for high morals. There is a need for more respect of persons. There is need for responsibility in our cities. There is a need to return to values that respect life and liberty.

Okay, let's say this is all too "preachy" for you. What part of *love your neighbor as you would love yourself* is confusing? What part of *honor your parents* is foreign? Which of the parts of *you should not murder* is aloof?

A criminal is one who does not want to be a part of society. A criminal is a predator of the weak. A criminal is a parasite. A criminal has chosen to be against those who follow the rules. Criminals should not be celebrated, protected, or encouraged. We have collectively lost our way or our "Tao."

We have great power that we squander. We have influence that we belittle. We give what we are responsible for to opportunists (politicians, actors, and clergy) and wonder why things are as they are.

Today many go after gun owners and those who promote gun rights in the name of peace, as if they are searching for witches in Salem in colonial Massachusetts between 1692 and 1693, when more than 200 people were accused of practicing witchcraft or the Devil's magic. Like the Witch Trials, those who go after gun shops and the firearms industry have become synonymous with paranoia and injustice, yet the current witch-hunt continues with the help of ignorance and fear, supported by rich big city mayors.

The Second Amendment witch-hunters protest outside of gun stores. They demonize law-abiding people trying to make a living. Interfaith groups like "Heeding God's Call" and some small churches that operate near gun stores often target the highly regulated federal businesses in a new form of Inquisition. The Reverends Jesse Jackson and Al Sharpton have been notorious for this type of action in the past to draw attention to themselves at the cost of the law-abiding. In the name of peace, they have tried to bait, entrap, or do some illegal act that can be caught on film. It is sad.

Violence in any form is wrong and against the law. using the term "gun violence" as a platform shows the naiveté and blind faith of the participants. All law-abiding gun owners are against violence. All law-abiding gun owners feel akin to the losses of life that occur when criminals commit violence against others. But, unfortunately, law-abiding gun owners are accused of being criminals just for owning guns. They are maligned because they are easy targets. The drug dealer in front of the crack house or the meth factory in the neighborhood probably has more guns than the store, but no one wants to confront that guy.

Unfortunately, in the name of faith, law-abiding gun owners have their characters assassinated without due process. Groups like Heeding Gods' Call and other ambulance chasers take advantage of victims, survivors of violent crime, and punish the law-abiding. They use Christianity to abase Americans who submit to government-operated background checks and higher scrutiny than most of the inquisitors. By taking the assumed high road as a fundamental religious group in the name of peace, they infringe on the rights of respectful people for their version of the truth. In some lands groups like this are called zealots; in others they are called the Taliban.

The truth is that the gun businesses which are affected and highlighted unfairly in a recent *Washington Post* feature are the only legal way a firearm can come into a city. And so, after the sale, whether it is hours or decades, a gun used in a crime has a high probability of having originated from the only FFL store in the area. Statistics that point to one such shop are a non sequitur. Like the mom and pop hardware store that is all but gone today, gun store owners fight a wave of public opinion, statistics, and a culture that rarely supports their business. They need protests like these like you welcome ant bites.

Gun owners support the conviction of the criminal enterprise, because bad apples taint the image of US all. All of the gun shops that are being objected to have been around for decades. The government has made it close to impossible to start a new firearms business since the Gun Control Act of 1968. The shooting sports are the most regulated and restrictive sports in the United States, and the safest in comparison, but you won't read that statistic anywhere. Facts rarely find their way into the news today. Statistics can be made to support the author's opinion without any credibility. No one checks the truth of many of the accusations made. The editorials that do respond are on a different section of the paper, often weeks later.

The First Amendment is used too often to demean the Second Amendment. The witch-hunt continues. The Second Amendment is a constant target of those searching for money, power, or attention.

In 2003, the church voted my pastor out for a host of things that I never saw as his aide. The man who had mentored me and eventually taught me some aspects of how to be a pastor was fired. He was the first clergyman who had defended my pro-gun stance. It was a giant fiasco that was embarrassing and spiritually damaged my family and at least five hundred other people I knew. The disgruntled church elders even called the police and hired special police officers to protect them from me. They erroneously thought I might be a threat to them if they hurt the pastor or he told me to hurt them. That was one of the main reasons I left that church even though I was not accused of anything. I left them because of how they treated others. I left them for how they wanted to sit me down as a minister when *The Washington Times* printed the article on me on page three about my activism. The four off-duty federal officers who were hired to "watch" me during that horrible day they booted out the pastor were most likely former students of mine at the Federal Law Enforcement Training Center. After talking to them that day, I got the opinion from what they said that they were hired under an assumption that I proved false. They were different toward me after our conversation that day, to the unease of the trustees who hired them. I have learned to be wary of large, established, bureaucratic churches ever since. I am so glad salvation doesn't happen by church committee.

CHAPTER 6

What's in a Name?

THE **INTERNET WAS STILL NEW, BUT** I enlisted the help of a friend to get me a web designer to promote my first book and the cause of freedom. I wanted to be the guy who was called to talk to teachers about violence. I wanted to be the guy who talked to preachers about gun control. I wanted to be the guy who was called on to thwart 400 years of racist gun control. It wasn't time yet.

I learned that some things happen to us because we either like it or are comfortable with it. You won't change your situation unless you are uncomfortable with it. Blaming "the man" or "the gun" for crime, death, poverty, drugs, "fill in the blank," is easier than self-analysis.

"I have seen the enemy and it is us."

(Walt Kelly)

It was the days of America Online 1.0 and everyone had dial up. My website was amazing. It had flash. It had audio, and it was too early for any of that. It took too long to upload, and only big corporations saw my site. So, I overshot my audience. I was trying to get the attention of the firearms industry and of politicians who could benefit from my angle; but what it told them was that I was ahead of them and my services were going to be expensive, from the looks of my presentation. It appeared that I didn't need their help.

Blackmanwithagun.com was better than the National Rifle Association's site at the time. Whoops.

The name *Black Man With A Gun* was not without some drama. It would have worked well in the porn industry as well. It is now a registered trademark of mine. (The porn industry actually leads the way on the Internet and created the model for social media, broadcasting, and e-commerce. Before porn, the Internet was little more than shortwave radio, geeks, and technically savvy groups posting on bulletin boards. I studied the developers who were making millions with Internet cameras selling the illusion of sex. It took ten years before "webcams" were on every computer or laptop, and now on cell phones. What some teens do now, "sexting," originated in the porn industry and was very lucrative.)

I was wondering how to make web cameras work in the gun industry. YouTube answered that question, but I wasn't ready for that. And then when the domain registration ended, and I didn't have any money, I lost the URL. I used blackmanwithagun.net until I was able to purchase the (.com) URL but then lost the (.net) URL to a porn site that still has it.

Having the (IM) instant message name of "Black Gun" or BMWAG got me either unwanted sexual attention or car enthusiast queries. This changed over time. I became Kenn with two "n's" to give Dr. Ken Blanchard, author of the

44

"One Minute Manager" fame, a break. He had made a life of motivating and inspiring business types and didn't need my chaos. I was still trying to find my way.

The name *Black Man With A Gun* has had its high moments. In a restroom, while standing at the urinal, I was recognized as the owner of the website Black Man With A Gun by a computer-savvy man who had been able to download my grandiose site. I almost wet myself when he yelled out, "Black man with a gun!" A few men in the restroom, unaware of who I was, just thought I had a gun and hurriedly got out of there. I probably caused some anxiety, cramps, and bowel issues that day for more people than myself. As graciously as I could, I smiled, acknowledged him, and tried to finish my business with some dignity. He was almost to the point of slapping me on the back when he finally realized where we were and nodded himself and backed out of the restroom, praising my nerve. I learned it is hard to feel tough with your zipper open; I don't care who you are.

As the world was preparing for Y2K or partying because it was "1999," I was finishing up the first edition of this book. I had high hopes with this book. Nothing similar had been published since "Negroes with Guns" by the late Robert F. Williams thirty years earlier. This was a primer. It was an entry-level book I had hoped would allow a discussion to start between the races. I had hoped this would be sold in every African American bookstore and stand at the mall. I even dreamed Oprah Winfrey would take notice of this poor guy and put me on the show once.

Things didn't turn out as I had planned. I did succeed in publishing the book, thereby making me an author. I did get my book reviewed in the National Rifle Association's publication, *The American Rifleman*, meaning it may have been seen by over a million people.

I learned that fame and fortune don't go together. I don't even think they are cousins. My wife calls me the most famous broke guy she knows. After twenty years of marriage and surviving what we went through, I'll take that as a badge of honor. But sometimes in my mind, my failures seem to outweigh my successes. I think I move from extremes. At times, I suffer from an overabundance of optimism, and then, at others, an extreme sense of doubt that anything I do will ever work out. This book was like that.

Langston Hughes wrote a poem that reminds me of what happened called "Dream Deferred." Like a "raisin in the sun," I had a few seconds of light, but in the end, it felt like my dreams withered on the vine. Maybe it was not that dramatic, but at the time it felt like it.

The original pictures in the book were done by a brilliant photographer who was famous to everyone but me. He agreed to do the pictures of the firearms and some stills showing the examples of how to do certain things. I knew I was in a professional's place as soon as I entered his home. I had never been in a "studio" before, and this guy had an immaculate house that showcased his work. There was jazz music playing on the stereo that was piped throughout the house, and the studio was complete with backdrops and tripods, props and lighting equipment that made me think I had just walked into a Hollywood set.

We took some pictures for the cover, and I didn't realize at the time that the U.S. flag was facing the wrong direction. It fit with the ominous foreshadow and the imagery of a bearded black man in a long black coat with a scary black assault rifle. The only problem with all of that is that it scared away potential sales and didn't portray that the book was positive. I have since learned that artistic people should be overruled if they don't understand marketing. After getting my book edited, and printed by a generous donation from a cousin who was reveling in a new career in professional football, the cover prevented many from opening the book. African American book stores that were all the rage in the eighties and nineties shunned my book as "negative subject matter," although you could find books aplenty on prisoners, pimps, whores, and dope fiends.

I learned that firearms businesses in general are fearful of the media. Cameras, both video and still, are not welcomed, for the most part, at many ranges. So wanting to take pictures for my book was another set of challenges. Fortunately for me, the owners of On Target Indoor Range in Maryland, for which I have fond affection, allowed us in to do just what I needed for the book.

I wanted the pictures of women in my book to illustrate how it might look to defend yourself from a home invader, as well as close-ups for how to properly hold a pistol or stand in the marksmanship section. My photographer friend got the help of a neighbor who I think was into something I wasn't. She came over to take photos in a Fredrick's of Hollywood ensemble that pulled my wife out of the car where she was waiting. She followed "sistergirl" in and protested her use. The "model" was then used in only one photo and strategi- cally placed behind a bed, where only her face and hands are seen. It turned out okay. My wife became the model for all the rest of the pictures where I wanted someone to demon- strate a particular stance or mood.

The photographer and I had a good friendship going until I bought him some mints. It was one of the awkward mo- ments that seem to happen to me more than to other people. In the beginning of our friendship, I noticed the guy was really particular about stuff, efficient and professional. I was glad but also realized I couldn't afford him. I thought the least I could do was to be as nice and considerate as I could manage. If you are a "Star Trek" fan, you may understand if I tell you that I identify with the Klingons. I have to work at being nice. I am generally nicer to animals than I am to people outside of my family. Anyway, I noticed he liked chocolate mints. After a barrage of Girl Scouts converged on me the week before at the shopping mall, I bought a box of mints. I thought the mints would be a good token of friendship. A week later, the opportunity presented itself as I was watching my photographer buddy explain the joys of shooting difficult people as he was developing the film he had shot for my book. I whipped out the gift bag I had made with the box of chocolate mints and told him I was thankful for what he was doing for me. I don't know how it sounded, but he took it like a solicitation. He was a little angry. It caught me off guard. Even my explanation didn't seem to work. Awkward! I think we are cool now, but I went back to my normal gruff ways. I learned men are funny about that sort of thing.

My cousin, the football superstar, loaned me the money to print my book and start my firearms business. I ordered five thousand copies and waited for shipment to come in. Five thousand 5" x 7" paperback books weigh one ton. When the tractor-trailer arrived at my suburban Maryland home, the driver was scratching his head. He knocked on my door and asked me where was my help. It was January. It was just beginning to snow, and I was alone. I took the day off and unloaded a tractor-trailer pallet of fifty-plus boxes.

Sales were slow for the first book. The cover design was too artistic. It was too scary. The Columbine tragedy was still in the minds of people when I was walking around from store to store to see if there was any interest in selling my book. My first sale of a complete box came from Gun Owners of America and the Second Amendment Foundation's Gun Week. Today, Larry Pratt and Joe Tartaro are still very special to me. I sold a few at church. I sold a few through my mother, who, surprisingly enough, at first didn't agree with my subject matter. "Where did all this gun stuff come from, baby?" I remembered her asking. "We didn't go to the range or have guns in the house," she said. It didn't take long for me to remind her my favorite toys growing up were the guns of any movie character. I reminded her about the Daisy Red Rider BB gun I got when I was nine years old. How it was my most treasured possession growing up. I reminded her that every summer, when she took me to stay with my grandmother in the land where I was born, a very rural part of southeastern Virginia, Grandma had a loaded shotgun in the kitchen, a pistol in her bedroom, and most of my core values came from her. The shotgun was loaded and unlocked all my life. It was never misused or touched by any of the grandchildren because of the respect for our grandparents and the responsibility she instilled in us. It was a short conversation. I could see the light go on in my mother's head as she processed our past with our present.

Despite what she had heard on the evening news, she realized I had lived in the same paradigm as her mother. I was an old soul. I didn't believe in the myths about gun control that were purported on the evening news to people who live in the city. I had missed the mantra that blamed the gun for the violence in the city. I was a disciple of an earlier time in America where everyone had a firearm in the home and nobody batted an eye. It was a time when little boys couldn't wait to grow up to be able to be given a pocket knife, a rifle or shotgun, and then a car. She became my best seller at her church. It's nice when your mother has your back.

In May 2000, I got the opportunity to meet and talk to American actor, iconic figure and activist, Charlton Heston. He was one of the best speakers I have ever had the opportunity to befriend. I only spoke to him twice, but the last time was the most memorable, as he shared some private stuff with me that made me appreciate him as a person. Not everyone who is on television or in the movies is worth a damn. Some are just playing themselves, getting overpaid for it, (in my honest opinion), and believing their own press clippings. Mr. Heston showed me a real guy who had gone through life not only imitating historical figures but learning from them as well.

The first time I met him, I was receiving the National Rifle Association's Carter-Knight Freedom Award for my work in the urban community. Mr. Heston looked like a man weathered by longevity, politics, and the past. But that was only until he walked toward the microphone and into the light of the stage. Like Clark Kent transforming into Superman, this old thespian straightened his back, lifted his head, and spoke with the same authority as Cecil B. De Mille's Moses from Mount Sinai. I don't know if he had memorized his lines or ad-libbed, but it was one of those moving and motivating speeches that kept him president of the National Rifle Association for as long as it did. The old dude was cool.

As I age, I hope somebody says at least that about me when it's my turn. Yes, he said some fiery stuff on occasion, irked people like Michael Moore, and even scared the NRA when he spoke his mind; but I respect a man who isn't out to please everybody. I respect a person who is not politically correct but truthful and passionate. I respected Charlton Heston. And he will be missed but never forgotten. When he was becoming the president of the NRA, and later became their most famous president, his staff used to send out autographed Christmas cards from him to me. Because I liked him so much, I used to send him one back. When he passed away in 2008, I mourned his death like the passing of a relative. Few people get those kinds of tears from me.

In 2004, I got the call from Lion Scotland for BBC Four to be on a 2005 television documentary called *Dickens in*

America that followed Charles Dickens's travels across the United States in 1842, during which the young journalist penned *American Notes*. The British actor Miriam Margulies, whom I recognized as Professor Sprout in the Harry Potter movies and from numerous cartoon voices, hosted the show.

In 2005, I got the chance to be in another documentary and meet with Larry Elder. *Michael & Me* was an independent, self-financed 2005 DVD documentary created by Los Angeles-based radio and television talk show host Larry Elder. His documentary attempts to disprove statements made by filmmaker Michael Moore in his 2002 documentary *Bowling for Columbine,* about the relationship between American culture, gun ownership, and increased violence.

In 2006, I was invited to appear as a guest on Cathy Hughes's cable show "Sharp Talk with Rev. Al Sharpton" on TV One. The new half-hour talk show hosted by Rev. Sharpton took place in Levels Barbershop in Brooklyn, where the good reverend talked about issues in the time-honored tradition of talking issues, politics, and culture in African American barbershops. The set of the show is in a former barbershop turned studio, next to a Karate studio and some really decrepit buildings in the 'hood of Flatbush. There was a platoon-size number of troops around the block setting up lighting, providing security, and doing Hollywood stuff. Two RVs acted as lounges and make-up staging areas in front of the place. It was impressive. Most of it you couldn't see from just driving by.

I finally got a chance to be the villain on TV that I had always wanted to be. I should have worn a black hat. For some reason, I always thought it was more fun to be the bad guy in the movies than the hero. You knew you were going to get it in the end, but that didn't matter to me. After fourteen years of representing urban gun owners as the Black Man

With A Gun in politics and social endeavors, being used in commercials, radio, and documentaries, I got the chance to be seen and heard by a new audience.

The subject of the show was Gun Control in Black America. It's a part I was born to play. I liked being the bad guy this time. The show aired in the latter half of 2007 and has been playing ever since on that station. I gave them two hours of material for a thirty-minute show.

I caught the plane to NYC's JFK airport, where a limo was waiting for me. Well, for that alone I was grateful. There had been fog, the plane was delayed, and I was having second thoughts the whole time. I rode through Queens, NY in the back of a Lincoln town car with a window that wouldn't roll up at first.

After few hours in the hotel, I was picked up and, during NYC rush hour, driven to Brooklyn –like a wounded bat out of hell. The ride down Atlantic Avenue wasn't scenic. After about an hour, the Reverend arrived and folks sprung into action with the makeup and stage prep. Knowing I was the antagonist in this opera was exciting. The bad part was, I wasn't ready for Rev. Al.

He started off cordially but quickly started his premise on fiction. To him and many of the people in earshot, "the firearms industry was the source of illegal guns in the Black community." To this panel, Liz, from Mothers against Guns/NY, and Marcus, AKA "DirtySeven" the rapper, the National Rifle Association was satanic. Most had never even heard of Eddie Eagle, a program for child safety education.

I got beat up pretty well because I had to answer or deflect questions that were posed wrong before I could provide truth. It made me seem ambiguous. Questions like "Do you still beat your dog?" for example cannot be answered with a "yes or no" and leave you held in high esteem. You have to restate the question and change the thing. I did that for the first few minutes, but not very well.

On the second wave I had to defend the NRA, which I didn't do for my own credibility's sake. However, it didn't come out as smoothly as I wanted. I did do a better job near the end of the dialogue to explain myself. It was a three against one fight.

Gun control is an issue that has affected Black America since before America was officially formed. Since 1640 AD, the effects of racism, the law, and the lack of education about firearms have been our demise. As a race, I think we accept defeat too easily. We want to shift the responsibility to someone else. We as a whole prefer to blame some force greater than we for the murders of our children, babies, and sons, rather than on the people who hate themselves, have no respect for life, or are void of responsibility. That was my first point. It didn't go over well. I ended up looking like a sanctimonious Black Republican.

I eventually caught my second wind and became comfortable in the fight. I started to interrupt and comment more frequently, instead of waiting to respond to crazy comments. By the end of the talk, I noticed that the barbers in the background were totally into my responses and no hair was being cut.

There is a hunger for knowledge in NYC that showed me that anyone knowledgeable about personal protection, firearm safety, and education has a ripe audience in the Big Apple. The problem is getting to them. You won't make any money on the deal, but you will do some good.

With this crowd, and I mean crowd, I said some stuff that wasn't as positive or polished as I know I could have been, but I wanted to show that I cared and wasn't a "tool" of the NRA. So there are a few quotes I am sure they will keep in the show that sound like I agreed with Rev. Al.

However, I left happy after the two-hour attack because of how it ended. The fifty or so people who were behind the scenes of a movie production like this practically clapped and gave me the thumbs up when it was over. I had caused them to question what they know. They wanted to learn more about their rights. Of my adversaries, Rev. Sharpton took off promptly to speak somewhere, but the other two exchanged numbers with me (Mothers against Guns of NY and a rapper from Brooklyn) and agreed to stay in touch. I learned that nothing and probably none of the people with a continued presence on TV are really as they seem.

In 2007, I remade the website and tried my hand at podcasting with a show called "Black Man With A Gun Live!" When I was child, I used a tape recorder I got for Christmas to narrate my comics. I loved broadcasting and wanted to get into it later, until I found out how cutthroat it was. The broadcasting business didn't fit into my life-style. I didn't have a degree in journalism or communication, had not done an internship for free at some radio station to work my way into becoming the on-air talent to create a persona that you hope would keep or make the ratings to survive the next Arbitron data dump. If your rating dropped, the stations dropped you. It wasn't until "podcasting" was created in 2005 that people like me had any hope.

CHAPTER 7

The NRA

"Never doubt that a small group of committed people can change the world. Indeed, it is the only thing that ever has."

- Margaret Meade

YOU'VE PROBABLY SEEN IT; IT'S red and blue text on a white vinyl bumper sticker. You might even have one on your vehicle that says, "I am the NRA."

Today, that would make you a minority. I've been a minority all my life, so I know a thing or two about it. I bet you've never thought of it that way before. Being part of a group with the same goals and the same core values is cool. There is power in numbers, and when you can focus that same power, there aren't many people who can stand against you.

It's like the difference between a shotgun and a 30-06. Both are long guns, shoulder-fired weapons; one disperses its ammunition scattered and over a relatively short distance, but with force strong enough to make almost a ten-inch hole. The second can travel thousands of feet and hit one target with enough force to knock it down. Each has its purpose. Sometimes we have to redefine our purpose, understand what we have, where we want to go, and what we want to do. The hardest thing about being part of a group of over a million people is that we don't all have the same goals, core values, or traditions. I am talking about the National Rifle Association.

At least once a month a new gun owner finds me and asks me, on my site, blackmanwithagun.com, if he or she should join the NRA. They will tell me they heard that only rednecks and racists belong to the NRA, along with some story about how the first person they met in a gun store or a range pissed them off so bad while wearing NRA memorabilia. I always surprise them with an answer: "I am the NRA." I wasn't always a member, though, so I understand. Their fear and perception are based on a public portrayal, stereotypes, and an abundance of ignorant people.

It's like that lie that all black men eat watermelon, play basketball well, and are physically well endowed. Well, even if one out of three of the comments is favorable, it's a stereotype. And that doesn't make it right for an entire population. Perceptions, stereotypes, and curiosity made me want to see this NRA for myself; and I'm glad that the night I went out investigating, I met the right people. I had been to several schools getting my credentials to become a firearms instructor, and my government managers frowned on my joining the NRA because of its political leanings. I wondered what the NRA was about for myself; I had heard so many negatives, and then there were the people who help that image. You've seen them. They wear the camouflage clothing and look like Larry the Cable Guy, or at least his cousin, or one of the lost members of the Beverly Hillbillies. It's that image America loves to make fun of, and the NRA is wrongly attached to it.

If you think you are cosmopolitan, or an accomplished person, and are ashamed of your rural roots, or even your heritage, you're going to have a hard time with it. But it's not just white people who fight negative images like that. I've got issues with young black men with their boxer shorts showing, trousers sagging down, prison-pet style, tattoos in places even sailors wouldn't put them, looking like carica-tures of the proud people they should be representing. We all have our pariahs.

You are looking for the truth, right? I knew that because if you seek the truth, the truth will make you free. I became an NRA firearms instructor in the late 80s; but when I crashed this NRA board of directors meeting, it was back in 1991. I found out that it was being held not too far from me in Virginia, so I walked into the hotel ballroom at cocktail hour with my usual attire: leather jacket, jeans, and cowboy boots. I'm a biker, what can I say. But now I was in a room of black ties and after-six wear. I wasn't sure I was in the right place, actually. Where were the flannel shirts and the camouflage? Where were the confederate flags and the spit cups? Saying I was inappropriately dressed is an understatement. I had done worse; I had fallen for the stereotype. My mindset was racist.

Racism is the belief that a particular race is superior or inferior to another, that a person's social and moral traits are predetermined by his or her inborn biological characteristics. It doesn't matter what color you are, because we all can be and are racist up to a point. In America racism developed be-cause of institutionalized slavery, which was accomplished because of the racist belief that Black Africans were less hu-man than white Europeans and their descendants.

The NRA was born from a racist country and culture. It is American. It has grown, matured, and evolved like everybody else. It is different today than it was in 1873. Was the U.S. military once segregated? Yes. Do people prefer to be in groups of people who look like they do? Yes. Is this natural? Yes. Is the NRA racist, not as an organization? Are there racists in it? Probably the same percentage as in every other organization. When I started this journey I was cautious. I had heard the same things most African Americans have heard. I have been ignored in the old gun shops with the Confederate flags and the deer heads on the wall. I have associated the negative stereotypes I have seen with the NRA because these were their ambassadors. These were the men who had "I am the NRA" stickers on their bumpers along with NASCAR and sexist references to women.

I have watched the NRA change over the past twenty years. The change was happening before I became aware of it, and probably before I was born. The NRA is just like the men who created it in America, with its traditions, cowboys, hunters, tycoons, and politicians. The NRA is still fighting stereotypes, embracing change, moving to correct deficiencies to remain viable, strong and healthy.

I have been privy to some unique meetings. I have been the only black male in the room. And although it was awkward, the only reason I was there was because I believed the folks who invited me were not racist. I shouldn't have been there, because I didn't bring anything to the table. I was in a room with CEOs of Fortune 500 companies, lobbyists, politicians, journalists, and wealthy people. As much as I would like to think I was representing the interest of all the African Americans who hunt, shoot, collect, and own guns, only my wife knew where I was. At best I was a symbol of what it could be if African Americans were united in anything, but truthfully we are divided on almost everything.

As a group of people, the Africans in America have been conditioned to favor the oppressor, black or white. When given the opportunity to change, some still reject it. The people we listen to are entertainers. It is sad. We still collectively vote, buy, and act based on irrational, emotional, and popular notions that make us pawns instead of players in a society of takers. We are preaching things which seem like good ideas but are not based on common sense. It is never economically prudent to trade in, give away, or turn in a firearm or family heirloom for a gift card or a pair of tennis shoes. Gun buybacks are insulting. Are we too stupid, irresponsible, or incapable of taking care of ourselves still? You'd better ask the outcast in your family. They are those poor souls who defy the stereotypes. It is these outcasts you see at the gun shows. It is these outcasts you see at NRA annual meetings. They are usually veterans. They are trained marksmen used to dealing with other people. They are academics, most likely college professors like Dr. Robert J. Cottrol and Raymond T. Diamond. Some are black nationalists. They have changed the names their mothers gave them at birth to ones of African heritage. They may be Islamist, Garvey-ites, members of the original Black Panther Party for Self Defense, followers of the Deacons for Defense and Justice. They know their history. And they probably scare white people. Then there are the security professionals, law enforcement officers in the family who have worked with diverse groups of people and carry a firearm every day. And mixed in with this stereotypical group of people who might be pro-gun and African American are the victims of violence who have decided not to be victims again. They took it a step farther and became liberators and street evangelists for the right to keep and bear arms. If you are trying to start a club of African Americans, or to bring some into your club, look for these archetypes.

When I entered the board meeting of the NRA, I saw a couple of senators, an African-American college professor I recognized from television, and a boatload of lawyers. How could I tell they were lawyers? I was a cop; I can smell a lawyer. But after the sensory overload, I headed for the door I had walked in through, embarrassed by my stupidity. Thank goodness I was stopped by two board members who took the time to explain what gave me a subtitle to what I was seeing. It changed my life. I was introduced to the association in the best way possible: personally. I was informed what the gathering was about and given information I was ashamed I didn't know, dealing with gun control and my own black history.

I learned that the NRA was formed in 1871 because two Union veterans of the Civil War were bummed out by the lack of marksmanship shown by their troops. The primary goal of the association would be to promote and encourage rifle-shooting on a scientific basis, as it was considered then. So basically the country boys outshot the city slickers.

My uncle used to say that if you don't know your past, you can never succeed in the future. These guys whetted my appetite for American history. I learned that after being granted a charter by the state of New York on November 17, 1871, the NRA was founded. Civil War general Ambrose Burnside, who was also the former governor of Rhode Island and a U.S. senator, became the fledgling NRA's first president. An important facet of the NRA's creation was the development of a practice ground. In 1872, with financial help from New York State, a site on Long Island, of all places, on the Creed Farm, was purchased for the purpose of building a rifle range. Named Creedmoor, the range opened a year later, and there the first annual matches were held. Political opposition to the promotion of marksmanship in New York forced the NRA to find a new home-force range. That stuff is still going on. In 1892, Creedmoor was deeded back to the state, and NRA matches moved to Sea Girt, New Jersey.

The NRA's interest in promoting the shooting sports among America's youth began in 1903, when NRA secretary Albert S. Jones urged the establishment of rifle clubs at major colleges, universities, and military academies. By 1906, NRA's youth program was in full swing, with more than 200 boys competing in matches at Sea Girt that summer. Today, youth programs are still a cornerstone of the NRA, with more than one million youth participating in NRA shooting sports, events and affiliated programs of groups like 4-H, the Boy Scouts of America, and the American Legion. Due to the overwhelming growth of NRA shooting programs, a new range was needed. General Aman B. Critchfield of Ohio had begun the construction of a new shooting facility on the shores of Lake Erie, 45 miles east of Toledo. Camp Perry became the home of the annual national matches, which have been benchmarked for excellence in marksmanship ever since. With thousands of people competing annually in pistol, small bore, and high-powered events, the national matches are one of the biggest sporting events held in the country today.

Now, through the association's magazine, *The American Rifleman*, members were kept abreast of new firearms bills, although the lag time in publishing often prevented the necessary information from going out quickly. In response to repeated attacks on the Second Amendment, NRA formed the legislative affairs division in 1934. Meanwhile, the NRA continued its commitment to training, education, and marksmanship. During World War II, the association offered its ranges to the government, developed training materials, encouraged members to service plant and home guard members, and developed training materials for industrial security. NRA members even reloaded ammunition for those guarding war plants.

Incidentally, NRA's call to help arm Britain in 1940 resulted in the collection of more than 7,000 firearms for Britain's defense against potential invasion by Germany. Britain had virtually disarmed itself with a series of gun-control laws enacted between World War I and World War II. After the war, the NRA concentrated its efforts on another much needed arena for education and training: the hunting community.

In 1949, the NRA, in conjunction with the state of New York, established the first hunter education program. Hunter education courses are now taught by state fish and game departments across the country and Canada and have helped make hunting one of the safest sports in existence. Due to increasing interest in hunting, NRA launched a new magazine in 1973, *The American Hunter*, dedicated solely to hunting issues year-round. NRA continues its leadership role in hunting today with a youth hunter education challenge, a program that allows youngsters to build on the skills they learn in basic hunter education courses.

Hunting is still an important aspect of the NRA, but you can't tell that by what you hear today. While the NRA did not lobby directly back in the 70s, it did mail out legislative facts and analysis to members whereby they could take action on their own. In 1975, recognizing the critical need for political defense of the Second Amendment, NRA formed the Institute for Legislative Action, or ILA. In 1978, a guy by the name of Neal Knox moved to Washington DC in order to lobby against gun control measures and started working for the National Rifle Association. He would go on to serve four years as executive director of ILA. At NRA, Knox was instrumental in convincing friendly lawmakers to introduce a reform of the 1968 gun-control act. The bill became the Firearms Owner's Protection Act, which eventually passed in 1986.

When I first met Neal Knox, he was old school. He was a bit gruff. I think he thought I was a waiter when I first saw him in a meeting, and that offended me. I think his use of the words "colored" and "gal" did something to me, too. You know how some people just rub you the wrong way. He wasn't alone back then. I was a stranger to these events, and these old white guys were products of the times. I got the same feelings from Col. Jeff Cooper and *Soldier of Fortune* guy Lt. Col. Bob Brown. Over time, Neal and I actually became friends and spoke at a few Gun Rights Policy Conferences together on the same panels. He was a country gentleman. He was actually a brilliant guy, a great family man, and a person you could respect. He didn't play. He wasn't liked that much by some of his peers in the NRA, I found out later, because he called it like he saw it and didn't toe the party line. I think he was actually ousted at an NRA board meeting in a hostile takeover, but I was young in the organization and not privy to all the juicy details. I just knew there was some bad blood between someone in the group and Knox. And by the time that was happening, I liked him, so anybody who was against Neal I wasn't going to turn my back on. It's how I operate. It doesn't matter how we start but how we finish. If I call you a friend, then I'll go to war with you if you need me. It just wasn't the best introduction two guys on the same side should have had. Neal's sons are carrying on his firearm tradition now online. They are a lot quieter, though, and a lot more Internet-savvy. They are good guys doing good things with their father's legacy. Of all the old timers, one guy I never got warm and fuzzy with was Col. Jeff Cooper, (may he rest in peace). Even being a former Marine, I couldn't give him any love. I must have caught

63

him at his worst (every time) and I'll just leave it at that. Of all the old guys, Bob Brown is cool now but still as feisty as ever. I like him. He has stories that will make your sides hurt from laughter. They all are/were board members of the NRA.

Now that I've bashed the old guys, let me explain what I have learned from them. Do you have grandparents who are still living? I don't, but I remember my grandparents were always old to me. That makes sense, doesn't it? They were two generations back; they lived in a different time. They were coming up and struggling during the Great Depression, grew up right after slavery was abolished, survived Jim Crow, the civil rights era, and a whole bunch of wars and personal poverty issues. Computers kind of messed them up; they never really owned one. They knew nothing about the stuff we take for granted now that hasn't always been here. Stuff like video games and cell phones, large-screen TVs, DVDs, mp3s, CDs, microwaves, Macs and PCs. They didn't trust people readily, and they were really reserved. And they had been through some stuff.

Well, that is the National Rifle Association. It's huge, it's old, and it's been around. And its management and the people who operate its boards of directors are grandparents for the most part, and they're dragging around their traditions. Tradition is a monster by itself. Tradition is strict; tradition is slow to change. Change is slow, change is cautious, change is treated as suspect. Remember, this group has been kicking since 1871; and it survived the Spanish-American War, World War I, World War II, Korea, Vietnam, the civil rights era, the gun control act of 1968, the 70s, the 80s, the Brady Campaign, and the Clintons. (With the exception of ILA, and ILA is the younger, rebellious and arrogant upstart, like me sometimes.) Anyway, you got to give it up for an organization able to last that long. Marriages don't last that long, corporations don't last that long. Yeah, it's got some issues.

And why? Because you and I haven't fixed them yet. You see, I am the NRA. I got a history with them, too.

I like that line from *Jerry Maguire* when he says, "You had me at hello." They had me when they gave me media training to allow me to be a spokesman for my people to keep me out of trouble. They had me when they helped me show a group of 30 inner city African-American gun owners that they were cool by allowing US to shoot on a brand new range they had built in their Fairfax, Virginia headquarters. They had me when they worked with me to help change laws so that all law-abiding people across the country, regardless of color or affluence, could carry concealed. They had me when I saw all the Asian and African-American, Hispanic, or other so-called minorities working in the headquarters and behind the scenes to get the stuff we get. They are the 800 pound gorilla in DC fighting for the right to keep and bear arms. Politicians love to hate them. The media can easily stir up people against them. Are they fast? No. They move at the speed of grass. Are they perfect? No. Have they made some tactical mistakes? Heck, yes. Are they racist? No. And I'll say, brother, they're more like a civil rights organization than you realize.

As Janet Jackson says, "What have they done for you lately?" Well, the NRA actually earned high praise for their amicus work on the Heller case, including the largest con-signed congressional brief in US history. They filed suits attacking gun bans across the U.S. within 24 hours of Heller and have already won against San Francisco public housing; Wharton Grove, Illinois; Nestor City, with the first total gun ban in U.S. history. We are still in suit against Chicago, Oak Park, Evanston, and Winnetka, Illinois. I think Winnetka is negotiating to drop their ban. When New Orleans P.D. de-clared that they would confiscate all guns in civilian hands after Katrina, NRA got a temporary injunction in days and fought for 3 years to get a permanent injunction, which was just obtained on August 27, 2013. We have filed suit against the state of Washington for discriminatory practices towards lawful aliens' ability to possess guns. We won a suit before the Ohio State Supreme Court in August, 2013, to prevent local gun bans and are involved in Cleveland's suit against Ohio over the same issue. Recently NRA helped get all the charges dropped by Cleveland against a young black man who lawfully defended himself with a gun over a year ago, and the Cleveland police tailed him and harassed him for months because he exercised his right to protect himself. We are in suits in a dozen other places to see that decent folks who choose to own guns are not persecuted for it. And we are in legislation across the U.S. and federally to keep governments focused on predators and not on regular citizens.

The NRA is required as a bulwark against gun-grabbers nationally and globally, even if they don't meet all your expectations. Without them, some future liberal enclave will be having a discussion of all the times the state has disarmed the populace and left them defenseless, and U.S. history will just be one more of those examples. I know we don't often see the NRA big picture. In everyday life, decisions are made that the average Joe doesn't think make sense, and that's because we don't know the whole story. The bottom line is: the gun-grabbers hate and fear the NRA, which means the NRA is obviously doing something right. We don't hear Schumer, Brady, Kennedy, Feinstein, Boxer, you fill in the blank, complaining about Gun Owners of America, or Jews For the Preservation of Firearms Ownership, much less any other pro-gun organization. The thorn in their side is the NRA.

When I got involved in the NRA around 1989-90ish timeframe, I thought the NRA inside was split into two realms. It probably still is, but don't tell them I told you so. There are the hunter/shooter programs and all the other stuff I just mentioned, and then there's the political part, ILA. To me, almost 99% of the gripes and complaints you have or hear originate from the ILA side. The begging for money, the selection of political candidates, the hiring and the brutal firing of people in the organization, probably come from ILA. Politics is big business in Washington DC; that is where the money begged for is spent. The parts of the association that train and provide help for the members take a second seat to this group. When you call and don't get an answer, it's because they probably fired the person who could have answered your question or picked up the phone. This is also the savviest part of the organization. This is the suit-and-tie group. They don't hunt or shoot like the other part as much. They work 12-hour days lobbying, wining and dining. It's more like an intelligence organization, if the truth be told. They hold the purse strings, so money is really tight within the entire organization. It costs a lot to advertise, to publish, and to keep up with all the personalities against the rights of gun owners across the United States, and now the world, but they do it. And, unfortunately, it's a shotgun approach. Sometimes the money is spent well and sometimes it's not. Sometimes the right people are in power and sometimes not.

If you are a hunter, collector, or recreational shooter, you may not be a fan of Washington politics and the corruption that happens around the Beltway. You probably also don't like bottom-feeding lawyers, lobbyists, or government bureaucracy. You probably don't want your NRA money used to pay salaries to suits. It's necessary, I am afraid, if you want to preserve what you do with firearms. In the midst of all that's going on, there are dishonest groups trying to capitalize on this growing rift among gun owners who think the NRA has left them. This conflict represents the best opening in years for anti-gun and politically savvy people to blunt the effects of the gun lobby, or ILA, on a national level. Conquer and divide tactics worked in war and still happen in politics. Be wary of that.

Groups have been formed to try to put a wedge between you and the NRA. They make alliances with anti-gun politicians, anti-gun groups, and anti-rights millionaires. Why? For the money. Or maybe even for revenge because they were once members of the NRA and things didn't get done or things were too rigid or too extreme.

There have been plenty of groups formed since 1871 to replace the NRA. They haven't succeeded in replacing its effectiveness or in defending our right to keep and bear arms. They've got some really close facsimiles; I mean they really look alike. They should be able to work, but they don't. We have pretenders and false prophets; we have haters, debaters, and assimilators. There are pseudo pro-gun groups and folks you know deep in your heart are just trying to capitalize on the chaos, the dissatisfaction, and the poor management of the NRA. It's like when you and your wife are having marital problems and, God forbid, you separate. Separation's supposed to be a time where you think about how good it was and how much you love each other and how you should reconcile, but what it has become now is a step out the door. And while you're out there you meet somebody and, in no time in all, start up a new family, a whole new set of problems, personalities, and sexual partners. That is all too much drama. When it comes down to it, all you really wanted to do is shoot, right?

Who knew to be a gun owner you had to be sensitive to diversity, a good communicator, and an above-average member of society? That is why I think the gun community is great. We have to step up and be better than our neighbors. We have to vote. We have to discern what the talking heads are saying. We use the Internet like the Underground

Railroad to send freedom, speak truth, and inform one another.

I even started a group once and learned quickly how much it required and that I didn't have it. It survived without me, and that is a good thing. Is the NRA perfect? No. But it is better to be part of something you can fix, improve, and update. Change happens best from within. Collectively, we've got it. We just aren't focused enough. Teamwork is the ability to work as a group toward a common vision, even if that vision becomes extremely blurry. You know, it's estimated that there are 80 million gun owners in America -- I'd like to see half of them become NRA members. Is it reality? No, but I can dream.

Should you join NRA, you ask? Yes. They are misrepresented culturally in some media. They seem like a cult to some, but they represent what made this country free and the people who know it takes money to keep a machine like that going.

You don't have to own a firearm to participate in the sport of shooting, but you should value your freedom. The National Rifle Association promotes the simple fact that all law-abiding Americans have the right to keep and bear arms, any arms. And they don't cut corners or mince words over which firearms are safer or better for you to own.

Since numbers mean power in politics, the NRA is constantly recruiting new members. You should join because life is not a spectator sport. I believe you should support causes that help you. Is it a perfect organization, no, but they are fighting for your rights, rights you may not care about today but which are yours just the same.

I am a member of the National Rifle Association, Law Enforcement Alliance of America, the Second Amendment Foundation, and Gun Owners of America. I am probably missing a few that claim me.

There is probably a pro-gun organization in your state right now that needs you. That group needs your participation. Not only will you find a worthy organization to spend your time with, but also you will find a like-minded friend who can pass an FBI background check.

CHAPTER 8

History

AFTER YOU DECIDE TO CARRY A firearm for your personal protection, you will enter a world that's older than you. Guns have been around since the beginning of gunpowder. It's a political argument. It's an evergreen subject. There are people who come into the fight on one side or the other. They will soon be against you, even though you've done nothing to them. Historically, those in power make the rules. Those in power do not want to see an armed peasant. The same thing is happening with firearms ownership today. As soon as you decide you want to buy a firearm for yourself, for your self-defense or for your hobby, you are now involved in an argument. The argument is over Right to Keep and Bear Arms (RKBA), or the Second Amendment (2A), or the actual type of firearm a regular person should be allowed to have. Magazine bands, assault weapons, you'll soon find out that there are people who will say they agree with you, but they don't. Some will only agree with the ownership of a certain type of firearm. Some believe that nobody should own a fifty caliber. Others are against the ownership of military-style sporting rifles. And you can't forget those who think nobody should own an assault weapon. And they all have their own reasons. Many of those reasons are unfounded by proof or any standing other than personal opinion; but those who are in power, their personal opinion sometimes sways law and other people. If you own a firearm for hunting, you are just as culpable and just as much in the fight for the right to keep and bear arms and the Second Amendment as the person who is only shooting their .38 on weekends. You are also equal with the person who is now shooting competitively at the international pistol and shooting competitions. You are also on par with the person who is big game hunting in Africa. You are also in the same street with those who shoot fifty calibers at a thousand yards. You are also on par with those who shoot .22s on the weekends only in the backyards of their farms. We are all in it together, no matter what you shoot. What will surprise many of you is that the white man and the black man and the yellow man and the brown man are all on par when they are firearms owners. Each one of us has to defend the other, because none of us is as strong as all of us.

The truth, however, is that black people or anybody of color, yellow or brown, have had a history of racism as it relates to guns, again, because firearms have been controlled. Peasants aren't supposed to have guns. Slaves cannot own guns. So, America has a history of racist gun laws I would like to tell you about right now.

Gun laws have been an issue in America since the Thirteen Colonies were formed, and the issue will not go away tomorrow. Gun control has been a part of my history since my grandmother's grandmother arrived. She is responsible, like many others, for the continuance of our family that was enslaved in the United States. I apologize that I cannot honor her name, because I don't know it. It is hard to trace the genealogy in my family because my grandmother's grandmother arrived in Virginia around the 1600s, when she was considered a thing. And it took some time, even after the Dred Scott Decision was passed in the mid-1850s, for black people to be considered human or citizens of the United States. She was among the many who survived as human cargo from across the Atlantic. You know the story; and if you don't, you'd better ask somebody. As a woman who did not speak the language of the colonists and could not hide because of her skin color, she adapted. To save her sons she made sure they would not touch, look at, or think too hard about owning a gun; because of the laws, to do so would be certain death. This tradition is ingrained in many black people.

Virginia's first gun law came out in 1640, preventing any black person from possessing a firearm. Fearing that a slave might either avenge himself or start a rebellion, laws were passed in every state that allowed slavery. The fear was so great to the slaveholders in power that they wrote laws that even possession of a can or anything that looked like a weapon was grounds for any Louisiana colonist to be able to legally beat down a black person. These laws were also known as the Louisiana Black Codes. They were copied throughout our country. So, when you see a white person who is protesting for the right to keep and bear arms and is trying to get people of color to be involved in protests or marches or any rally, you should be there. You have a chance to be their star, to go against 400 years of oppression. Free men own guns; slaves cannot.

The Constitution of the United States is a not a holy writing like the Torah, the Koran, or the Holy Bible; but like these books it has been misquoted and interpreted for the benefit of the speaker. The debate about gun control begins with the Second Amendment.

The U.S. Constitution was written to guarantee that all Americans would have freedom from tyranny and injustice. Congress passed the Second Amendment on September 25, 1789. It was ratified by three-fourths of the states on December 15, 1791.

This amendment did not apply to non-whites at this time; this kind of inequality is evident in the time lapse between the writing of the Constitution and the ratification of several amendments. It took some time from the conception of the Constitution before slavery was abolished with the Thirteenth Amendment, even though the words "all men are created equal" were inscribed on the original document. Americans of African descent didn't get their full right to vote until the Civil Rights Act of 1965.

The first Supreme Court case to bring up the issue of Second Amendment rights involving black men with guns was called Cruikshank v. United States. Two African American voters, Alexander Tillman and Levi Nelson, were murdered in Louisiana, c.1875. They were either going to, or coming from, the polls when attacked. Posses of deputized African American men had to barricade themselves and hold off a vigilante attack. The Cruikshank case focused mostly on the violation of Tillman's and Nelson's right to vote and their right to assemble and have freedom of speech, but there was also the issue of their right to be armed. The court found the group of whites guilty of thirty counts of conspiracy.

After President Lincoln issued the Emancipation proclamation in 1863, and after the Thirteenth Amendment to the United States Constitution to abolish slavery was adopted, and the civil war ended in 1865, states still prohibited blacks, now free men, from owning guns under the laws called Black Codes. And they did so based on the idea that

74

black citizens did not have the same rights as whites, including the right to keep and bear arms protected in the Second Amendment to the United States Constitution. This was specifically articulated by the U.S, Supreme Court in the Dred Scott versus Sanford decision in 1857. The U.S. congress overruled most portions of the Black Codes by passing the civil rights act in 1866. The legislative histories, including both the Civil Rights Act and the Fourteenth Amendment, as well as a special report on the anti-slavery conference in 1867, are full of denunciations of those particular statutes that denied blacks equal access to firearms. After adapting the Fourteenth Amendment to the U.S. Constitution in 1878, most states still placed a neutral business or transaction tax on hand gun purchases. However, the intentions of those laws were not neutral. Those taxes kept poor whites and former slaves from being able to afford to own guns. And it's still kind of the same thing now; with the prices of firearms being as high as they are, you have to almost sacrifice a rent payment to be able to buy a firearm. The economy today still makes it difficult for the poor to legally buy a gun. In Florida, for example, in 1825, there was an Act so that slave and free black homes could be searched for gun confiscation. (Act to Govern Patrols as 1825 Acts of Florida 52-55 section 8) It said that white citizen patrols shall enter into all Negro houses and inspect their places and search for arms and other offensive or improper weapons and may lawfully seize and take away all such arms, weapons and ammunition. Section 9 provided that a slave might carry a firearm under the statute either by means of a weekly renewable license or if in the presence of some white man.

So, back to my family again. The women in my family would have done everything possible in their power to protect the lives of their kids, to save us, keep us out of jail, or keep us from being hung from a tree, so they would not allow firearms in their homes. They would have forbidden us from owning a firearm even for self-defense. Gun laws in North Carolina made it a crime for anyone in my great-grandmother's home from even carrying a gun, for fear that it might frighten people. My family resided in the Tidewater area of Virginia and surrounding areas of North Carolina, where actually Nat Turner's rebellion took place in 1831. Virginia's response to Turner's rebellion prohibited the ability of free blacks to carry or keep any fire-lock of any kind, any military weapon, or any powder or lead; and it was so bad that a black family found possessing even lead shot used as scale weight was considered a sufficient reason for a frenzied mob to contemplate summary execution. And that's why I use the phrase "Black Man with a Gun," to cause a knee-jerk reaction to Americans of African descent. The title of my website alarms more people of color than anybody else who has inherited the taboo and the dysfunction with freedom. Descendants of institutionalized slavery have not been legally free for that long. As a matter of survival, black families have been conditioned by terror not to be armed.

So, when the Civil War ended, President Andrew Johnson permitted several southern states to return to the Union, but he did so without guaranteeing equality to blacks. These states enacted those Black Codes I spoke about and decided to keep ex-slaves in de facto slavery submission. White terrorist organizations like the Ku Klux Klan attacked freed men who'd stepped out of line, and Black Codes ensured that the freed men could not fight back. We were forbidden to own or bear firearms and thus rendered defenseless against assaults.

Back to economics, small pistols selling for as little as fifty or sixty cents after the Civil War became available in the 1870s and the 1880s, since recently emancipated Americans, both poor whites and blacks, could afford them. Changing the price of a gun by ten cents was enough to cause economic hardship back then. This was allowed due to the significant threat to a southern establishment interested in maintaining the traditional class structure.

In 1870, Tennessee banned selling any but the army and navy model handguns, much more expensive. They were beyond the means of most working class people. In 1881, Arkansas enacted an almost identical ban on the sale of cheap handguns, while in 1902 South Carolina banned the sale of handguns to all but sheriffs and their special deputies. In 1893 and 1907 Alabama and Texas respectively put handguns out of the reach of Africans and poor whites through heavy taxes on sales. After the turn of the century, gun laws changed to persecute another group. The passage of gun restrictions against the foreign-born, especially those from eastern and southern Europe, was illustrative of this. From the 1880s to the mid-1930s, the new immigrants to the U.S. were greeted with fear. Almost all the states passed laws prohibiting ownership of firearms by aliens.

In 1911, New York City passed the Sullivan Law, the most restrictive gun law of its time. Not surprisingly, the city's businesses fought hard to favor this law, alleging it was a means to reduce the crime rate. This law had especially obtuse clauses related to aliens that made it a felony for them to possess a weapon.

During the Jim Crow Era around 1900, when racial oppression was at its peak, several states enacted handgun registration and licensing laws. As one Florida judge explained, the laws were passed for disarming the Negro laborers and were never intended to be applied to the white population. At first it was relatively easy for non-white or for white non-aliens to obtain a permit to own a firearm, and at one time as many as 35,000 permits were issued. Now it's almost impossible for a regular citizen of New York City to obtain such a permit. Interestingly, the first person to be arrested and convicted under the Sullivan law was an Italian immigrant.

Indeed, a close perusal of *New York Times* articles concerning the Sullivan Law for the period of 1911 to 1913 indicates that over 70% of those arrested for the violation of this law had Italian surnames. Predictably, during this period of anti-Italian ethnicism, it was almost impossible for people of Italian descent to obtain weapons permits in New York City. From the onset, the Sullivan Law did not reduce homicide and other weapons-related crimes.

It did, however, give the police a sufficient pretext to arrest undesirable aliens, especially those anarchists and radicals who were suspected of being involved in labor unrest. The early operations of the Sullivan Law provide us an example of the major political implications of interdictionism; such laws can be selectively enforced in order to carry out political or ideological goals.

Gun control laws that are seemingly non-discriminatory and apolitical can be selectively enforced against persons who constitute a threat to the government. And this continued on through the early twentieth century, where weapons prohibited or Prohibition surfaced with the bans on 'suicide specials' or 'Saturday Night Specials.' This term originated from an Ohio writer who noted that he wished he could party like a nigger did on Saturday night. He wrote that the only downside was that blacks killed each other recklessly with cheap handguns while partying in his particular Ohio suburb on Saturday nights. So, in his opinion, it was not safe for a white person to club among the indigenous population because it was nigger time Saturday night. The term 'Saturday Night Special,' coined in reference to these cheap guns, stuck and is still a common phrase today. Any reference to cheap, affordable handguns as 'Saturday Night Specials'

78

is racist. The African American population in the south of the country was effectively disarmed and suppressed until the 1960 Civil Rights movement. The new assaults on civil rights participation caused some brave brothers to arm themselves, which did stop many of the Klan terrorist attempts. In an effort to protect the leaders and participants of the nonviolent struggle of the sixties, African American men organized into an armed militia, based out of local churches and called "The Deacons for Defense and Justice." Created in 1964, secretively and without a formal structure, they kept their community safe from attack because they took a vow that if they were shot at, they would return fire. They set up armed patrol car systems in cities such as Bogalusa and Johannesburg, Louisiana, and completely succeeded in deterring Klan and other attacks on civil rights workers and black residents. As many as sixty chapters of the Deacons were formed throughout the south during this time. Of the more than one hundred civil rights workers martyred in the 1960s, almost none was armed.

My grandmothers were of a different mentality. Both of them favored shotguns and rifles and kept them loaded in their homes to protect us from harm and to get the occasional meal. They were both hunters. They both lived in the same general area of Tidewater, Virginia, and in the early part of their lives realized the importance of self-reliance and self-defense, even though it meant going against what was preached publicly to black people.

Gun control and its enforcement are the strictest in areas around the country where there are people of color. Name a city! If there is a large number of people of color, the gun laws will be strict. Where are the most violent parts of the United States? The cities. Have our gun laws saved anybody yet? No.

I advocate the arming of all law-abiding, responsible adults who want to.

One of my grandmother's fears came to light in 1968 in New Jersey, when criminals stole military rifles from a National Guard armory. The National Guard violated the rights and ransacked the homes of forty-five families without a warrant to search for their missing weapons. They found none in those homes and left the houses in shambles. The murders of President John F. Kennedy, Malcolm X, Martin 'The King' Jr., and Robert Kennedy justified the passing of the Gun Control Act of 1968 to many people. Gun laws are a mess. It is really easy to be lawful in one place and criminal in another. There should be reciprocity of concealed carry and gun ownership equal to a driver's license. Now it's a glob of grey areas that anyone who intends to be a lawful gun owner has to wade through.

The Gun Control Act of 1968 changed the way dealers are defined, mail order is done, and people are allowed to give gifts to friends and family. Like all laws, these are created, put on the books, but never go away. This act has also changed and increased the political involvement of the National Rifle Association. It wasn't always a political organization. People who promote gun turn-ins, gun buybacks, junk guns, or suits against firearms companies are not so foolish as to openly promote racist laws; but when they say their gun control ideas and motivations are colorblind and unbiased, they are lying. You must remember that the reasons for disarming Americans are the same today as the ones used 300 years ago in the time period of my great-grandmother. It is the self-serving career politician or businessperson who regards law-abiding Americans as childlike creatures in need of guidance from politicians or masters. It's a fact that racism is so intimately tied to the history of gun control in America that we have a problem that won't go away overnight.

Prior to the National Rifle Association's creation of the Institute of Legislative Action (ILA), they had political stuff on the run, until a deluge of prohibitive laws emerged in the 60s and 70s which encouraged them to change their standing. When the NRA changed their stance from a hobbyist organization into a lobbyist social force, of course there were problems.

Politics within the organization between gender and age still haunt the place, as it does in any big corporation. The National Rifle Association is not the only game in town. There are a good handful of very large pro-gun organizations you can affiliate with, but you should probably join them all, because each has a different flavor and has a different purpose. Historically, let me give you a couple of instances of black men involved in the right to keep and bear arms.

In 1925, Dr. Ossian Sweet moved into an all-white suburb of Detroit, Michigan. The police failed to restrain the mob that threatened his home, and a white man was killed by somebody from his house. Dr. Sweet and his family were charged with first-degree murder. He was later acquitted after a lengthy trial, had to move, and had many threats on his life. Lawyer Clarence Darrow defended him and became a Supreme Court judge. Troubled the rest of his life, Dr. Ossian Sweet, I believe, committed suicide.

In 1966, a mob burned the headquarters of the W.E.B. Du Bois Club while the New York police looked on. When a club member fleeing from the burning building pulled out his pistol to hold off the mob, the police arrested him for illegal gun possession, and nobody in the mob was arrested for anything.

I've already mentioned the 1968 National Guard Armory being ransacked or robbed in New Jersey. In 1976, Armistan Spencer moved into a white neighborhood in Rosedale, Queens in New York. Crowds would dump garbage on his lawn, his children were abused, and a pipe bomb was thrown through his window. When he responded to a menacing crowd by brandishing a gun, the police confiscated the gun and filed charges against him.

In the nineties I worked with the NRA in several states testifying for the right of concealed carry in places where people who looked like me didn't normally get approved by the state to carry a firearm for their self-defense. After that success, I worked on trying to save my family and my career and entered the ministry. There are a few other notable spots in history of which I have firsthand knowledge, however.

In 2003, I believe, I met two guys from the Cato Institute looking for a resident of the District of Columbia. I introduced them to someone whom I had just met, Shelly Parker. She ended up being a plaintiff in a lawsuit seeking to overturn the ban on firearms useful for self-defense in the city. Prior attempts to change the gun laws had always been thwarted by legal technicalities or political corruption in DC. In 2004, Sandra Seegers found that out in her case, *Seegars v. Ashcroft.*

In *Parker v. DC, the CATO Institute organized a* diverse group of plaintiffs to represent the District of Columbia. There was the ordinary citizen who wanted to own a handgun for self-defense; Dick Heller was a Special Police Officer licensed to carry a handgun while working but not at home, (who additionally applied for a license to do so, but was denied); and then there was a gay man who has been assaulted for his sexual preferences but had in the past defended himself from assault with a handgun; and Shelly, a legal gun owner in DC who was forced to keep her self-defense gun disassembled and inoperable.

In 2004, I got the call from Lion Scotland for BBC Four to be on a 2005 television documentary, *Dickens in America,* that followed Charles Dickens's travels across the United

States in 1842, during which the young journalist penned *American Notes*. The show was hosted by the British actor Miriam Margolyes, whom I recognized as Professor Sprout in the Harry Potter movies and as numerous cartoon voices. I brought the actor into my new church to hear me deliver a prayer and serve the minister there before taking her to a nearby range for instruction and her first shot. She was deathly afraid of firearms, but I successfully got her to fire two rounds from a .38 caliber revolver. She was a sweetheart of a person, even though she admitted she didn't believe in my God or my guns. Admittedly, she did like me and my spirituality. We eventually traveled to New York for a special screening and to meet many of the other interesting people she visited as the updated "Dickens figure" coming to America. It was an odd and eclectic group assembled that day in downtown New York. She purposely had me sitting next to a lesbian minister who led a congregation somewhere. I guess it was for effect. However, I doubt if I "performed" as she expected. I am sure the event was recorded as well, although I didn't see it played anywhere here. The BBC played the documentary *Dickens in America* back in Great Britain, where it gained the attention of all the pro-gun people of Europe and the former British colonies. Soon afterwards, I received invitations to visit France, Holland, New Zealand, and South Africa. I became a cult figure in Papua New Guinea. At the time of this writing I have yet to visit any of those locations, but it is nice to be asked. I learned that everyone learns at a different pace; and even if I can't change someone's mind instantly about guns, safety, and responsibility, at least I can contribute to it. It is a lot like evangelism. Some plant, and some may water, but it is God who causes the increase.

In 2005, I got the chance to be in another documentary and to meet with Larry Elder. *Michael & Me* was an independent, self-financed 2005 DVD documentary created by Los Angeles-based radio and television talk show host Larry Elder. His documentary attempts to disprove statements made by filmmaker Michael Moore in his 2002 documentary *Bowling for Columbine*, about the relationship between American culture, gun ownership and increased violence. I received an email from the "Sage of South Central" radio talk show host Larry Elder, asking if I would be willing to be in his upcoming pro-gun film in a few months. I had heard of Mr. Elder but didn't know too much about him. I had read one of his books after our conversation to get a gauge on what I would be dealing with and thought that although older and more educated, he was dealing with the same issues I was: trying to make a way out of stereotypes, conditioning, and preconceived notions of right and wrong. The worse issues you can confront are those of your own family and community. I could tell from the people I polled about him that Mr. Elder's greatest critics were those of the African American community. I agreed to be in his film and gave him the location of a place I thought would be a good backdrop for his filming.

A few months later, when he called me to see where I was, I had almost forgotten about the appointment we had made. When I arrived at the Associated Gun Clubs of Baltimore outdoor range there was a full film crew waiting for me. Larry quickly admonished me about being on "C.P. time." "C.P. time" is that colloquialism for when non-Europeans arrive late to events, appointments, etc. We call it 'Colored People Time," but I have also heard it referred to as "southern time." In my travels I have noticed that it happens in more than the African American culture. I believe it may actually come from cultures that have no drastic change in season. Europeans, on the other hand, may have had to move faster because of the climate, harsh winters, and short

84

growing seasons, causing them to be more time-sensitive. I have noticed, and have no scientific proof, that cultures that originate from places where it's warm or hot tend to move slower even as we evolve into a commonly accepted form of business or government. My reasoning didn't excuse my tardiness. Larry continued to share that he had mortgaged his house to fund this project, that all the people I saw holding cameras, reflectors, and microphones were on his payroll, and I was costing him money. Ashamed and repentant, I thought the best thing I could do was be the best I could be for his recording. I proceeded to go into character as the Black Man With A Gun. Highly animated and charismatic, I told my story and answered his questions. The editor later called me and said that they kept most of my recording because it was so good. All I had wanted for Larry was for his documentary to succeed. He sought to counter the negatives of the millionaire Michael Moore, and the disparaging comments he had made about freedom, the Second Amendment, and my friend Charlton Heston. The film didn't do so hot, but it placed somewhere in the film festival he submitted it to. It seemed at the time, the topic of his show was a common thread, and not the only film of its kind, so it didn't win. I am not sure if Larry recouped his losses for the project, but I got to meet a nice guy. I learned how expensive filming is. I learned the importance of time and honoring your word. I learned that being right doesn't mean you will win a fight or a cause.

A friend of mine is the namesake plaintiff in an important upcoming U.S. Supreme Court case originating from the "Parker v. District of Columbia" that some people don't want you to know about. On my birthday in 2008, the Supreme Court affirmed, in a 5-4 decision, the ruling of the U.S. Court of Appeals for the DC Circuit in *Parker v. District of Columbia* (re-cast as *District of Columbia v. Heller* before the Supreme Court), that the Second Amendment protects a pre-existing, private, individually-held right to keep arms and to bear arms without regard to a person's relationship to a militia. The decision struck down the District's bans on handguns and on having any gun in operable condition as violations of the Second Amendment; and it prohibited the District from denying plaintiff Dick Heller a permit to carry a firearm within his home on "arbitrary and capricious" grounds. The Court held that the Second Amendment does not (as the District argued) protect a right to possess arms only while in service in a militia or (as others have argued) a "state's right" to maintain a militia.

This professional African-American woman just added her name to the likes of Cruikshank, Dred Scott, and Ossian Sweet, in that she as a person of color is defending in court her right to legal self-defense. This "gun control" argument is important to us because it seeks to undo a historical precedent: the racist practice of making the places in the United States where there are more people of color more restrictive if you want to protect yourself. In states where there are fewer so-called minorities, citizens can get a permit to carry a concealed firearm without hassle. What this does prove in statistics, crime reports, and in quality of life testimony is that the ability to carry a concealed firearm lowers crime and provides for the general welfare even for non-gun-owners. Criminals don't rob people where they have the chance of being injured. In states which allow their citizens to carry legally, they don't have Wild West shootouts, nor does everyone chose to carry. What it does is give you a choice, and a better chance.

2009 Second Amendment March

I was a part of The Second Amendment March in 2009. It was a gigantic undertaking. While there are millions of gun owners, most are divided into certain groups. The organizers had hoped that marches held all over the country would rebuild a grassroots awareness of the principles of the freedom and remind gun owners of the need for solidarity. I got involved because of my spiritual support of the whole thing. I just wanted them to succeed. I have found in my years of pro-gun advocacy that the little guy never gets support from those he should. You will more than likely end up in the end underfunded, maligned, and beaten for trying to do something on your own. I know because I sought financial help as well, hoping to reach the people you don't see at a NASCAR race but who enjoy and support the shooting sports. For months I prayed for and with members of the Second Amendment March team. I helped as much as I could without sounding annoying as the official podcast of the March. I reminded my listeners about it, played ads for it, and fielded questions.

We had about 3,000+ total over the course of the day. Had they not had local and state rallies so close in time, been so close to Tax day and the Tea Party rallies, and if it had been on a weekend, I think it would have been huge. I read Illinois alone had seven rallies linked to the Second Amendment March.

I was excited and afraid when asked to speak on the grounds of the Washington Monument. I live here. My church is here. I work here. If there were an adverse reaction to the March, or to my speech, the aftermath would be long. Aside from that, I wanted it to be my best speech ever. I enlisted the help of a writer to help me make my talking points succinct. I prayed for good weather and a safe day. The Sunday before the March, I opened the church up after the worship to receive some out of town guests and some of the speakers for the following morning. I had my friend and caterer prepare a buffet for the guests. We had a good time.

On the day of the March, I asked one of my ministers to escort me and keep me company for the day. I needed someone to comfort me and keep me focused on the task at hand and was glad he accepted. The March was well-attended. The National Park Service estimated over three thousand people showed up to the big stage on one of the corners of Constitution Avenue. I was extremely nervous, unlike most of the time when speaking, and I am not sure why. The crowd was the normal homogeneous pro-gun crowd, with a sprinkling of diversity here and there. I got the chance to meet Tim Schmidt, publisher for *Concealed Carry Magazine,* and Mark Walters, host of the Armed American Radio, before I spoke to an apprehensive crowd. Here's what I said:

Speech:

Good morning, ladies and gentlemen. It is a great day for supporters of the Second Amendment. I was going to say glorious day, but then you might think I was preaching. In church I do preach, but everywhere else I teach. I teach friends and strangers who don't know or don't know better about the Second Amendment.

And thanks to the First Amendment, I'm standing before you today to share my perspective on this hot topic, (confident in the fact that the Second Amendment has a core group of supporters behind it that will never let it be less than what it was intended to be ….the right to keep and bear arms).

You see, I know all about how people can interpret things in different ways. On my birth certificate it says colored; a few years later I was referred to as a Negro. In the seventies I was black. And then Afro-American. Ladies and gentlemen, please allow me to introduce myself: I am the black man with a gun and I am an American!

I'm proud to say that this country was founded by a group just like this one gathered here today…people who were willing to stand up for what they know is right. Now we are standing up to protect a right that others keep trying to modify for their own agendas.

If it were not for people like you, people who are committed to preserving the essence of the Second Amendment, then over time we would see others erode our freedom to the point where it would lose its original meaning, its essence, and its beauty. Let's keep America free!

This event is going to get a certain amount of media coverage, and there is going to be a full spectrum of opinions regarding the necessity of such a gathering. Some will say we are reactionaries, who pontificate for our own benefit. They will say we are misguided in our strident opposition to modifications to the Second Amendment because, they will say, modification to the Second Amendment is necessary to preserve a more peaceful society. And others will say we are doing the right thing, because if people like us don't stand up, then what we fear can happen to the Second Amendment will, in fact, happen. I am glad you are here to do the right thing!

How many people here pull a trigger of some kind? How many people believe that everyone in this great country of ours has the right to keep and bear arms? If you pull a trigger, then you should be aware of what events are taking place regarding the Second Amendment.

Whether you're shooting a moving target with a paintball marker, hunting big game with a rifle, taking your daughter to an indoor range, or simply have a firearm at home for self-defense, you not only need to be aware of current events involving the Second Amendment, but you need to be committed to preserving the Second Amendment.

We as pro-rights advocates need to band together – not as individual groups, but as one. We need to be one vote and one voice.

Don't be misled by the politicians. They have their own agendas. You might see a senator on a big game hunt and think he has our best interest in mind. And the next thing you know that senator is signing off on some new proposed form of gun control.

In case you haven't noticed, politicians are very good at dividing and conquering. This is why I want to reiterate that we need to be one voice and one vote!

You know politicians and a baby's diaper should be changed regularly, right? And for the same reasons!

So how do we become one voice? I urge the leaders of the firearms industry and gun owners to reach out to one another in order to create a more unified position. When we speak as one and move forward as one, they can't help but hear us.

I realize that this won't happen overnight. But we have to do it. If you are a competition rifle shooter, you can find a lot of reasons not to get involved with the indoor range crowd. You might think proposed restrictions on people in the city are not a direct threat to you in the country. And likewise, pistol shooters may perceive restrictions on .50-caliber rifle-shooters as no big deal or no threat to you.

And that is what the politicians are counting on. They want the diverse assembly of firearms owners to not act on each other's behalf. That makes it so much easier to legally steal your rights.

You see, our guns may not look alike or perform alike, but we are alike in that we all pull a trigger. By coming together, by rallying behind each other's causes, we can create a unified voice that starts off low and rises up ....like a choir.

Can I get an amen, somebody?

What is truly alarming to me is how unrelenting the opposition to gun ownership is. Be not deceived, they are clever. They are very good at portraying law-abiding gun owners as unsophisticated, backwards-thinking reactionaries who refuse to compromise with their notion of a peaceful solution. Do you know what my notion of a peaceful solution is? My right to keep and bear arms!

I enjoy the trigger sports. I enjoy everything that goes bang. I enjoy talking about them and sharing the knowledge and history behind their designs. I appreciate the fact that I can own a firearm. And there are millions of law-abiding citizens just like me, everyday people who use guns responsibly.

And yet we are grouped together with criminals. We are perceived as people who don't care about the safety of others. We are perceived as wrong in our steadfast commitment to preserving the Second Amendment.

Well, I got news for you. We are the ready citizens, the white and the blue collar workers who have helped make America the greatest country this world has ever known. We are the people who pull a trigger and save lives in the operating room. We are the people who pull a trigger and uphold the law in our courtrooms. We are the people who pull a trigger and pave our roads and build our buildings. We are the people who built this country.

We need to correct the false impressions of us with the truth. Do you know the truth will make you free? When the opposition puts us down, we need to stand up.

Another point I want to make is how the survival of the Second Amendment is reliant upon each new generation. As parents, it is our duty to pass along life lessons to our children. I suggest that in your long list of lessons, you include the Second Amendment. Personally, I'm not just talking the talk, I'm walking the walk. I have spent many hours teaching my son proper firearms etiquette. I've shared with him the history of firearms and the tradition of gun ownership in my family. More importantly, I've taught him how to be a responsible gun owner. As a result, he has developed respect for life and a healthy respect for the rights of others which someday I hope he passes on to his children.

One of the ways I support the Second Amendment is through my website, blackmanwithagun.com. Every week I have a podcast where I talk about various aspects of firearms ownership, gun control, and the news. I interview movers and shakers in the community and everyday people like you and me. This is my personal forum for keeping the Second Amendment in the forefront of the public's consciousness. This is a duty I feel compelled to perform, demonstrating my personal support for gun ownership.

As much confusion as there is in the general public about gun rights, there is an even greater misunderstanding in the city about law-abiding firearms ownership. We look at the violence perpetuated by troubled youth, gangs, and criminals, and seek solutions that go against the very civil rights our parents have died for. Many have forgotten that our ancestors here in America owned guns and used them to hunt, shoot for fun, and protect us from harm. Ignoring that truth, there are too many leaders who have developed a steady stream of sound-bites aimed at fanning the flames of fear. I use my website to include all people, to poke fun at myself and defy the stereotype.

The ultimate test of a government is whether it will allow its citizens to be armed. That is the only way you can truly tell if you are free. As a descendent of former slaves, who is now free, one point is very clear to me: free men own guns; slaves do not. It's time for all communities to move forward and enjoy the rights and freedom this country was founded for.

Freedom is having a choice to arm and defend yourself. That lesson I learned during my time in the United States Marine Corps. That lesson I learned serving as a federal police officer. That lesson I learned from being in the company of Americans like you, my fellow gun owners.

In closing, I suggest to you that we have to start making our politicians more accountable. It's time to put a stop to the flip-flopping, the special interest groups, and the votes for sale. We should prepare an agreement and individually present it to our local, state, and nationally elected officials. The document should have in writing that they agree to protect our Second Amendment rights. And if we don't get their signatures, then they don't get our votes!

It's time for our country to return to its most basic form... a nation for the people, by the people.

And, as I say at the end of the urban shooter podcast, Shalom, baby!

Thank you very much.

After my speech, exhilarated from the adrenaline still flowing, I worked the crowd and listened to the rest of the speakers for the day until the finale with Lucas Hoge, a Nashville singer closing it down in song. After the March, things went back to normal for me. I did get the opportunity to meet a few listeners of my Black Man With A Gun Show and the chance to write for other websites. Other than that, nothing changed.

By 2007, all the legal stuff was just known as DC v. Heller. The DC v. Heller decision marked the first time in its history that the Supreme Court had clearly established that the Second Amendment guarantees the right of gun ownership to individual citizens, rather than granting the states a "collective" right to form armed militias. What cities like DC, New York, and Chicago did directly afterwards was to create even stricter restrictions, since the District of Columbia is a federally-controlled district, and not a state.

The Urban Shooter Podcast began around this time and is still going strong.

In the case of McDonald v. Chicago around 2010, I had nothing to do with it. I didn't know the cool brother Otis whom the case is named after. McDonald, 76, says he had seen his neighborhood on the far South Side of Chicago turn from bad to worse over the years, with "gangbangers and drug dealers." All I know is that the Supreme Court ruled that the Second Amendment right to bear arms also applies against state and local governments. Otis McDonald, the man behind the lawsuit, said he had been robbed several times and wished to purchase a hand gun so that he could defend himself against criminals in the city. The decision was 5-4. The Supreme Court said that an individual right to bear arms and keep them in your home is a fundamental guarantee that was made by the United States and will remain the law despite other reforms local governments may have passed regarding the issue. Previously, the Supreme Court had shot down a local law that placed a handgun ban in Washington DC.

CHAPTER 9

Safety

I GOT INTO THE BUSINESS OF FIREARMS
instruction to save lives. Ignorance kills. Education got
my people off the plantation and living as free men
and women. We somehow missed the boat on continuing that

education with all things. Guns are one of those subjects.

From the time he or she picks up a firearm, the shooter
becomes a part of a system over which he or she has complete control. You are the only part of the system that can
make a gun safe--or unsafe.

Believe it or not, hunting and target shooting are among
the safest of all sports. You can help meet this responsibility by enrolling in hunter safety or shooting safety courses
at local ranges. You must constantly stress safety when
handling firearms, especially to children and non-shooters.
Newcomers, in particular, must be closely supervised when
handling firearms, with which they may not be acquainted.

Don't be timid when it comes to gun safety; the life you save maybe your own.

Below is a list of rules you will probably see each time you go to a public range; learn them. A more in-depth reason for these rules will follow.

1.   Treat all guns as if they were loaded.
2.   Always keep the muzzle pointed in a safe direction.
3.   Keep your finger off the trigger until you are ready to fire.
4.   Be sure of your target and what's beyond it.
5.   Always wear eye and ear protection when shooting.
6.   Be sure the barrel is clear of obstructions before shooting.
7.   Don't alter or modify your gun, and have guns serviced regularly.
8.   If your gun fails to fire when the trigger is pulled, keep the muzzle pointed in a safe direction.
9.   Use correct ammunition.
10. Learn the mechanical and handling characteristics of the firearm before you use it.

Treat all guns as if they are loaded. Unless used for self-defense, firearms should be loaded only when you are ready to shoot in the field, on the target range, or in the shooting area. Firearms and ammunition should be secured separately from each other and in a safe place when not in use. As a responsible gun owner, it is your responsibility to prevent children and careless adults from gaining access to firearms or ammunition. Unload your gun as soon as you are through. Whenever you handle a firearm, or hand it to someone, always open the action immediately and visually check the chamber, receiver, and magazine to be certain they do not contain any ammunition. Always keep actions open when not in use. Never assume a gun is unloaded; check for yourself! This is considered a mark of an experienced gun handler! Furthermore, never cross a fence, climb a tree, or perform any awkward actions with a loaded gun. Never pull or push a loaded firearm toward yourself or another person. There is never any excuse to carry a loaded gun in a scabbard, in a holster not being worn, or in a gun case. When in doubt, unload your gun.

Always keep the muzzle pointed in a safe direction. This is the most basic gun safety rule. If everyone handled their firearm so carefully that the muzzle never pointed at something they didn't intend to shoot, there would be virtually no firearms accidents. It's as simple as that, and it's up to you. This is particularly important when loading and unloading a firearm. In the event of an accidental discharge, no injury can occur as long as the muzzle is pointing in a safe direction. *Safe* means a direction in which a bullet cannot possibly strike anyone, taking into account possible ricochets, and the fact that bullets can penetrate walls and ceilings. The safe direction may be up on some occasions or down on others, but never *at* anyone or anything not intended as a target. Even when dry-firing with an unloaded gun, you should never point the gun at an unsafe target.

Develop safe shooting habits. Make it a habit to know exactly where the muzzle of your gun is pointing at all times, and be sure you are in control of the direction in which the muzzle is pointing, even if you fall or stumble. This is your responsibility, and only you can control it.

Keep your finger off the trigger until ready to shoot. Treat every gun as though it can fire at any time, regardless of pressure on the trigger. The *safety* on any gun is a mechanical device and, as such, can become inoperable at the worst possible time. Besides, by mistake, the safety may be *off* when you think it is *on*. The safety serves as a supplement to proper gun handling, but it cannot possibly serve as a substitute for common sense. You should never handle a gun carelessly and assume that the gun won't fire just because the safety is on. Keep your fingers away from the trigger while loading or unloading. Never pull the trigger on any firearm with the safety on the *safe* position or anywhere in between *safe* and *fire*. It is possible that the gun can fire at any time, or even later when you release the safety, without your ever touching the trigger again. Never place the safety between positions, since half-safe is unsafe. Keep the safety *on* until you are absolutely ready to fire. Regardless of the position of the safety, any blow or jar which is sufficient to actuate the firing mechanism of a gun can cause it to fire. This can happen even if the trigger is not touched, such as when a gun is dropped. Never rest a loaded gun against any object, because there is always the possibility that it will be jarred or slide from its position and fall with sufficient force to discharge. The only safe gun is one in which the action is open and which is completely empty. *You* and the safe gun-handling procedures you have learned are your gun's primary safeties.

Be sure of your target and what's beyond it. No one can call a shot back. Once a gun fires, you have given up all control over where the shot will go or what it will strike. Don't shoot unless you know exactly what your shot is going to strike. Be sure that your bullet will not injure anyone or anything beyond your target. Firing at a movement or a noise without being absolutely certain of what you are shooting at constitutes criminal disregard for the safety of others. No target or animal is so important that you do not have the time before you pull the trigger to be absolutely certain of your target and where your shot will stop. Be aware that even a .22 short bullet can travel over one and a half miles, and a high velocity cartridge such as a .30-06 can send its bullet more than three miles. Shotgun pellets can travel five hundred yards, and shotgun slugs have a range of half a mile. Shooters should keep in mind how far a bullet will travel if it misses its intended target or ricochets in another direction.

Always wear eye and ear protection when shooting. Everyone participating around a range should wear protective shooting glasses and some form of hearing protectors while shooting. Exposure to shooting noise can damage hearing, and adequate vision protection is essential. Shooting glasses guard against twigs, falling shot, clay target chips, and the rare ruptured case or firearm malfunction. No target shooter, plinker, or hunter should ever be without them. Wearing eye protection when dissembling and cleaning any gun will also help prevent possibility of springs, spring tension parts, solvents, or other agents from contacting your eyes.

Some handguns have hammer block safeties installed to prevent this; however, this caution applies to most shotguns. And most firearms don't fire from the open bolt position.

There is no protection, including condoms, that is one hundred percent effective all the time. You owe it to yourself to get the best you can afford. If you are shooting indoors or under a covered range, the risk of nerve damage is increased as the sound of gunfire bounces off the structure. If you are tired, fatigue also heightens hearing damage. The inner ear contains small muscles, called *stampedii*, which dampen the transmission of the loud noises to your inner ear. When you're tired, these muscles don't work as well. Hearing protectors are labeled with noise reduction ratings (NRR) and provide you with a number to compare brands. The ears cannot be toughened up. Damage to the ear is permanent.

Hearing protection NRRs are rated in decibels, (dB), the measurement of sound intensity. It is measured logarithmically, so that each increase of ten dB is ten times greater than the lowest figure. Normal conversation is at about sixty dB. A gun blast is about one hundred and forty dB. Anything over eighty-five dB is considered dangerous to your hearing.

FYI, a wad of cotton in your ears only reduces a gun blast by seven dB. The disposable foam plugs provide adequate protection outside and, when used with a hard earmuff, double your protection. The foam plugs, when used correctly, can give you an NRR of thirty to thirty-five dB, dependent on the brand. Earmuffs have a lower rating but protect the area around the ear. Sounds resonate off your skull and can be picked up indirectly. To help prevent flinching from the intimidating muzzle blast of some ammunition, use both muff and foam plugs. When shopping for gear, don't settle for what is rented. You can buy inner ear protection form-fitted by an audiologist; these work fairly well but don't do such a good job on rifle reports. There are kinds that fit behind the neck, have glasses and muffs together, and can fit all the different hairstyles. Earmuffs tend to get uncomfortable after a while, so shop accordingly.

Eye protection is another consideration to the shooter. Dust particles, shards of metal, and the residue after a bullet is fired are just some of the optical hazards possible. If you're at a public range, the threat of a hot shell casing coming over the partition on your head is common. If you wear prescription glasses, don't take them off to shoot. A simple clear plastic insert or clear wrap-around-style glasses found in drug stores will do. Glasses should be tempered glass or, preferably, high impact plastic.

Shooting glasses are available in a variety of colors and materials. Gray glasses darken the scene without changing color or contrast. Yellow lenses are intended for inclement weather to lighten and add contrast. Yellow tends to sharpen your vision, but since it is darker than clear, it may not be suitable for all indoor ranges. Bronze glasses add contrast but darken the scene. Red or vermilion glasses are used primarily for trip or skeet shooting. Try different styles and colors to see what is best for you and don't skimp on safety equipment; you only have one set of eyes.

Be sure the barrel is clear of obstructions before shooting. Before you load your firearm, open the action and be certain no ammunition is in the chamber or magazine. Then glance through the barrel, if possible, through the breech, to be sure it is clear of any obstruction. Even a small bit of mud, snow, excess lubricating oil, or grease in the bore can cause dangerously increased pressures, causing the barrel to bulge or even burst on firing; this can cause injury to the shooter and to bystanders. Make it a habit to clean the bore with a cleaning rod and patch to wipe away anti-rust compounds in the gun each time immediately before you shoot it. If the noise or recoil on firing seems weak, or doesn't seem quite right, cease firing immediately and be sure to check that no obstruction or projectile has become lodged in the barrel. Placing a smaller gauge or caliber cartridge into a gun--such as a 20 gauge shell in a 12 gauge shotgun--can result in the smaller cartridge falling into the barrel and acting as a bore obstruction when a cartridge of proper size is fired. This can cause a burst barrel or worse. You can easily avoid this type of accident by paying close attention to each cartridge you insert into your firearm.

Don't alter or modify your gun, and have guns serviced regularly. Firearms are complicated mechanisms which are designed by experts to function properly in their original condition. Any alterations or changes made to firearms after manufacture can make the gun dangerous and will usually void any factory warranties. Do not jeopardize your safety or the safety of others by altering the trigger, safety, or other mechanism of any firearm, and do not allow unqualified persons to repair or modify them. You'll usually ruin an expensive gun. Don't do it! Your gun is a mechanical device which will not last forever and is subject to wear. As such, it requires periodic inspections, adjustments, and service. Check with the manufacturer of your firearm for recommended servicing.

If your gun fails to fire when the trigger is pulled, keep the muzzle pointed downrange. Occasionally, a cartridge may not fire when the trigger is pulled. If this occurs, keep the muzzle pointed in a safe direction. Keep your face away from the breech. Then, carefully open the action, unload the firearm, and dispose of the cartridge in a safe way. Any time there is a cartridge in the chamber, your gun is loaded and ready to fire--even if you've tried to shoot and it did not go off. It could go off at any time, so you must always remember the first rule and watch that muzzle!

Use correct ammunition. You must assume the serious responsibility of using only correct ammunition for your firearm. Read and heed all warnings, including those that appear in the gun's instruction manual and on the ammunition boxes. Improper or incorrect ammunition can destroy a gun and cause serious personal injury. It only takes one cartridge of improper caliber or gauge to wreck your gun, and only a second to check each one as you load it. Use only ammunition that exactly matches the caliber or gauge of your gun. Firearms are designed, manufactured, and proof-tested to standards based upon factory-loaded ammunition. Hand-loaded or *reloaded* ammunition deviating from pressure generated by factory loads or from component recommendations specified in reputable handling manuals can be dangerous and can cause severe damage to guns and serious injury to the shooter. Do not use improper reloads or ammunition made of unknown components. Ammunition which has become very wet or has been submerged in water should be discarded in a safe manner. Do not spray oil or solvents on ammunition or place ammunition in excessively lubricated firearms. The residue can affect the primers of the ammunition.

Learn the mechanical and handling characteristics of the firearm you are using. Not all firearms are the same. The method of carrying and handling firearms varies in accordance with the mechanical characteristics of each gun. Since guns can be so different, no person should handle any firearm without first becoming thoroughly familiar with the particular type of firearm he or she is using, the safe gun-handling rules for loading, unloading, carrying, and handling the firearm, and the rules of safe gun-handling in general. Just as one example, many handgun manufacturers recommend that their handguns always be carried with the hammer down on an empty chamber. This is particularly true for older single-action revolvers, but it applies equally to some double-action revolvers or semiautomatic pistols. You should always read and refer to the instruction manual you received with your gun or, if you have misplaced it, simply contact the manufacturer for a free copy. The person with the gun in his or her possession has a full-time job. They must know how to use, handle, and store their firearm safely. Do not use any firearm without having a complete understanding of its particular characteristics and safe use. There is no such thing as a foolproof gun.

In the home, there are some additional safety rules and considerations. One is that firearms not under your direct control should be made inoperable or inaccessible to unauthorized people. I could never cover all the methods of storage possible for firearms since they will vary from household to household. What is good for one is inappropriate and outright dangerous for another. If you live alone, you might merely have to move your firearms to a covert place when you have company. A home with others may need to keep firearms locked up, unloaded, or both. The various storage options range from keeping the firearm unloaded and away from ammunition, merely disassembling the firearm, keeping it loaded but in an inaccessible safe or box—or any combination of the three.

One area for serious thought is homes that have children. Do you merely lock up the firearm or rely on your education of the children and their discipline to preserve safety? As soon as your child reaches the age of maturity and responsibility, safety courses are in order. They should be taught the basic safety rules, the understanding of how a gun works, and a graphic demonstration of how destructive your firearms could be, since the only images they have are what they and many of us see on television. And don't forget that an unauthorized show and tell could be fatal. Do not rely on your educated, well-behaved, disciplined kids to control their peers in your absence.

Basic firearms education should be given to everyone, especially in a household where firearms are accessible. A few minutes of education can sometimes overcome the fear of firearms. You have many options now in regard to securing your firearms. In addition to the many manufacturers who produce security items, you can make some firearms safer simply with the use of a bicycle padlock. A small *Master*lock can be placed around the frame of a revolver when the cylinder is open, which prevents the cylinder from being closed and/or fired. A cable lock can be run through autoloaders so that no magazine or round can be placed in the chamber. The cable trick may even work for the shotgun if used through the ejection port through the feed ramp. Try a few combinations to see what works for you. The keys could be kept with you, of course, and it's simple, inexpensive, and, if done properly, effective.

There are locking boxes, gunlocks that prevent the slides in autoloaders from going into battery, even audible trigger locks that prevent the manipulation of the trigger. Check out the new US RAC that allows you to bolt a lock anywhere.

What is practical and safe for you varies from person to person. Think before you act. As a gun owner, you represent all of us; and each mistake can cost us all our right to ownership.

CHAPTER 10

Children and Guns

CHILDREN BEING SHOT IN THE CIT-
ies is a tragedy that can be prevented. It can be
prevented the same way we prevent our chil-
dren from ingesting poison, playing with matches, or being
kidnapped by strangers. We train them. We work with them
individually and reinforce the instruction at every level.

Children learn that nine, forty-five, and twenty-two are
the names of handgun calibers long before they learn that
these same numbers are called *Arabic* numerals. Children
do not grow up in fear of firearms. They will not do the
safe thing without instruction. In the inner city, and in your
neighborhoods, the chance is high that your child may find
a discarded handgun or be able to obtain one on the black
market. You have the responsibility to teach your children
about guns before they learn about them through tragedy.
The teens in your house probably know where your firearm
is *secretly* kept.

These are the guns that are showing up in the classrooms, on the playgrounds, and on the street corners. As a parent, I try not to underestimate my child's curiosity. It is only through education and closer involvement with our children that we are going to save them. Education has always been the instrument of survival for our people. Silence from parents is contributing to the murder of our children. The child who grows up in a nurturing home is more responsible and respectful around all firearms.

Not everybody grew up in a household with firearms or the hunting tradition. I understand that. Parents who didn't grow up in the gun culture fear looking stupid, so they avoid it. Preachers who didn't grow up in the gun culture or chose to capitalize on the fear don't help by having gun buybacks in their churches. Those who fear angering "momma" perpetuate the mentality that they can just hide the gun in the house and it will be okay. Hidden is not secured.

In the summertime, children usually have twelve hours of freedom in a household to explore and discover. Firearms found by children without proper instruction are disastrous. You would think adults would have gun safety courses in schools, if for no other reason than to make sure all children would treat any firearm found in the absence of an adult as a dangerous mechanical device, but no. That fear is total. Those things that should not be named are not for us. We don't use them. Those things kill. The mantra is repeated until any gun owner without thick skin avoids it like the plague. The ignorance grows. Silence means consent. Until that silence is broken by gunfire, tears, and weeping. I have seen the enemy and it is us.

Long before the dramatic and tragic events of the Newtown, Connecticut, shootings, there were the Virginia Tech Massacre, the Columbine High School shooting, and similar tragedies where high school teenagers went berserk in Springfield, Oregon, and Fayetteville, Tennessee, killing classmates. In middle schools in Edinburgh, Pennsylvania, and Jonesboro, Arkansas, children and a teacher were killed by murderous youth.

Nonprofits seeking to support political candidates and causes use gun control. They are getting both wealth and good press for their efforts. These groups can't offer solutions but use each tragedy for their benefit. Local politicians use it to show that they can do something during their tenure. Legislatures pass more laws and force the firearms industry to enforce laws the government isn't able to. You cannot legislate human behavior.

"Gun violence" is a misnomer. You might see this more than once in this book. There is just violence. Just like being a little pregnant. The words "gun violence" indicate that if we rid ourselves of the mechanical devices called guns life would be perfect. There are no quick fixes when it comes to human beings. The answer to saving our children from self-destruction and anti-social behavior is a combination of three things which cannot be done in isolation but must be done in concert with one another to work.

Children need their parents to be more involved in their lives. For many people, this is a sacrifice they are not willing to live with. The result is the children in the court system. We have sacrificed them for better living and allowed strangers, the television, and entertainment to rear them. In comparison, a dog that has been tied up and isolated is not very social, either. It is territorial, hostile, and unpredictable. Humans left alone become the soulless monsters who shoot in playgrounds and school classrooms. These are somebody's children. We have done it to ourselves. If everyone could just take care of one child, preferable their own, we wouldn't have so many problems. We are so worried about fixing the world that we are letting our homes go to hell.

This problem has nothing to do with the government. The people who help our community don't run for offices. You know them, too. They are the strong sisters and brothers who care about their kids. They are those who know where their children are at one o'clock in the morning.

The second piece of the puzzle is education. Without knowing the facts, adults contribute to the mayhem that is caused. If you knew that assault rifles account for less than one percent of the crime in the United States, you would not fall for the anti-gun legislation as a fix for our problems. You would demand more education, enforcement of the thousands of laws already on the books, and you would take an active part in your child's education. If you were educated on the facts, you would know that having a firearm in the home does not seduce a sane person into committing suicide. If you are thinking of suicide, you have internal problems the gun has nothing to do with. Education was the sought-after element of my African ancestors in overcoming the legacy of institutionalized slavery in the United States. All my elders wanted was for us to become educated. Education is not found only in academia. You must learn how to survive day-to-day living. Somewhere in our quest for civilization we forgot to keep it simple. Firearms education should be the same as fire prevention, poison prevention, and requiring child safety seats in cars. Knowledge alone is not power. It is what you do with your knowledge that empowers. Some people fear that children educated about firearm safety, hunting, and marksmanship will become killers. I disagree strongly. If that were so, then learning about human reproduction and playing with dolls would encourage teenage pregnancy. Should we ban the dolls? Education rules. Adults and children, parents and teachers, should learn about firearms as if your lives depended on it.

Finally, the third element required to complete the process and stop the death of innocents is a belief system. For my family it is the Gospel of Jesus Christ. What do your kids believe in? In what do they put their faith? The street hustler believes in the same theories as the corporate raider. To the hustler, there is no right or wrong, no morals or ethics. Their belief is, just don't get caught. The kids on the streets want what adults want. They want wealth, power, and status. They weigh the risk of each crime as a chairman of the board would a legal merger, minus the maturity. These are the hopeless children who have made a frontier out of the streets we walk. They have lost all respect for their elders because their elders have lost respect for each other. They will kill for honor, just as feudal societies did in days gone by.

Supporters of gun control can quote all the statistics they want from other countries. Statistics can be made to prove anything. All the protests and midnight vigils in the world don't mean a damn thing, either, if we cannot be living examples to our children. If you want to save the children--be a parent. Nobody can fix it but us. If you choose to own a firearm or two, do the right thing: involve your family in a safety program. Don't take shortcuts with your safety. Find a real trainer and get formalized training.

Talk to your children about guns and violence. Explain that guns are not toys. Tell your kids that if they see a gun in a friend's house, they should stay away from it and inform you about it immediately. Despite what you think of the NRA, the *Eddie Eagle* program is a winner. It deals precisely with this issue, for young children. Below are my top three recommendations for things you can do after you get training in safe firearm handling.

   1. Get to know the parents of your children's friends. The more you know, the easier it is to spot potential danger away from home.

2. Encourage and be a part of your local school's efforts to develop a violence- education program that includes information about gun safety as well as conflict resolution.

3. Monitor what your kids watch on TV and in the movies. Young kids aren't able to distinguish between what looks like reality on screen and real life.

Remember, *you* are your child's primary role model. That is how we change things.

Civilized people are taught by logic, barbarians by necessity, communities by tradition; and the lesson is inculcated even in wild beasts by nature itself. They learn that they have to defend their own bodies and persons and lives from violence of any and every kind by all means in their power!

Cicero

CHAPTER 11

Shooting Sports

G UN OWNERSHIP IS FOR MORE
than self-defense. There are so many activities
gun owners can involve themselves in that I
couldn't even list them all. Each has its own type of targets,
course rules, distances, speeds, number of rounds, and gun.
There is something for everyone. Not only is shooting and
competing fun, but also there is money to be made. If you
can get your child interested in shooting competitively, you
can encourage her to do even greater things. Don't let the
fact that these competitions are almost exclusively patron-
ized by white Americans discourage you if you are a person
of color. I can guarantee the people you meet will be the best

people you have ever met.

All it takes to be a competent member of a shooting sport
is a firearm suitable for the sport in which you are partici-

pating, the right ammunition, proper training, comparable equipment, and knowledge—a little thing like knowledge goes a long way.

Your first task is to find out which event you want to try and do some research on that event. What type of weapon is commonly used? What are the rules of the competition?

You don't want to bring a revolver to a pistol match that requires fifteen shots to be fired in a specified time limit, unless you are the fastest speed re-loader in the territory. What equipment will you need? Is it a stationary bench match, action shooting, sporting clays, metal silhouettes, air gun match, skeet shoot, or Olympic trial? Is it indoors or out? What type of ammunition will you need? A pin match requires a special round that grabs the pin. Ordinary ball ammo tends to ricochet or glance off the same pin unless struck in the perfect place.

Hopefully, this knowledge will make new shooters search for events they can participate in and motivate the African American shooters who have been out there shooting in secret to take the lead, organize teams, and begin competing as a group. I started the *Tenth Cavalry Gun Club* in 1992 to gather people of color together who have traditionally been excluded from firearm ownership from fear or lack of exposure. While that seemed segregationalist, it was needed to overcome cultural taboos and centuries of conditioning.

We as individuals have much to offer the world if we just took the blinders off.

Literally, as long as you aren't too visually impaired, you can shoot; you don't have to be in great shape to do it well. It is a learned skill that requires discipline to master your weaknesses. However, it takes more than just eye and hand coordination to shoot well— of course, you need a gun. Fellow Christians do not fear this sport or gun ownership.

Having a firearm doesn't make you a killer, just as owning an ax does not make you an ax murderer.

Here are a few of the ways you can enjoy the shooting sports aside from just going to the indoor range and shooting a stationary target. I want to introduce a few terms to you to whet your appetite.

The term *action shooting* is used generally to mean any kind of fast shooting at multiple targets. These events also include the NRA action shooting sometimes referred to as the Bianchi Cup shooting event. This, of course, was named after holster maker John Bianchi, who first sponsored this sport.

Pin shooting is an outdoor event that uses bowling pins as targets. The objective is to shoot a specific number of pins off a table faster than anyone else. The caliber of choice is the .45 ACP, loaded hot with a 'big nose," a powerful round with a bullet-tip that can grab a pin. In order to move the heavy pins three feet back off the table, momentum is needed. Some shooters use the .38 Super or the .357- caliber that can contain loads with comparable bullet velocities. Whatever caliber you choose, bullet construction is important. As I stated earlier, pin-grabbing rounds work best. Pin grabbers are semi-jacketed hollow points with serrated edges that bite into the pin, even with edge hits.

Plinking is a term used to describe a non-competitive shooting sport where you go out in the country to a safe and legal area, set up your own target range, and begin *slinging* lead. It can be as elaborate as your purse will allow or as Spartan as a few tin cans. The object here is to have a various targets at various distances at which to shoot and to have fun.

Rimfire or .22-caliber ammunition is the most economical to use for plinking because it is the most inexpensive and easiest to replenish. Most .22-caliber weapons have a higher ammunition capacity, therefore allowing the shooter to spend more time shooting than loading. Plinking's biggest drawback is that you must have access to property on which you can shoot openly. The two-mile range of a .22-caliber long rifle round and the noise pollution make this hobby difficult for those who live in the city.

Speed shooting is like the drag racing event of the gun world, taking guts, money, and skill. Shooters fire at steel plates and silhouettes in timed events. In this competition, the plates don't necessarily have to be knocked down, just hit. For this reason, the caliber is smaller than for other events. The smallest cartridge is usually the 9- mm Luger. A range officer who records the number of shots fired and the time in hundredths of a second follows the shooter. There are matchers who utilize large optical sights, laser sights, special steel, and alloy guns. This type of shooting includes the IPSC (International Practical Pistol Shooting Confederation) matches, as well as the practical pistol courses utilized by many police organizations. IPSC shooters fire at various targets. Some are stationary, some bob, some are as close as two feet away, and some are as far as sixty yards. You shoot freestyle, offhand, weak hand, sitting, prone, behind barricades and barriers, and through windows.

Practical pistol shooting usually means using a police firearm that is typical of the one issued on duty. However, times are changing; many of these guns are now fine-tuned weapons that are so jazzed up they don't resemble the duty weapon of a law enforcement officer anymore.

Silhouette shooting is a sport utilizing the hunting handguns. Targets resemble animals like the chicken, turkey, wild pig, and ram. This sport originated in old Mexico, where cowboys used to put a goat or a pig on the horizon, stand back as far as they could, and try to shoot the poor creature. The first one to draw blood was declared the winner.

115

Today, the targets are life-sized metal silhouettes, except for the ram, which is slightly smaller than in real life. Shots are fired mostly from prone and kneeling positions at distances of as much as two hundred meters. Firearms used are usually the large-bore revolvers with six-inch barrels. There is a course, however, that utilizes the .22 calibers, appropriately called the small-bore hunter pistol course. The distances shot with these pistols are shorter and only go up to one hundred meters.

Not all shooting events involve handguns. The use of shotguns in sports has increased with the growing interest in sporting clays, skeet, and trap. Skeet shooting began as a way to practice bird hunting. It was a hunters' sport from the beginning. The shooters stand with lowered guns, mounting them only after the target is airborne, and the clays are released at any time after the shooter calls the familiar *pull*. Skeet uses crossing and overhead targets. The shotguns used have barrels of 26 to 28 inches long and are the same type used in hunting birds. A skeet gun is stocked to shoot flush, placing the center of its pattern on the point of aim. Most of these guns contain chokes that help hold the pattern. Skeet ranges are semicircular points in which the clay discs, called birds, are shot in stages. These clay *birds* are domed saucers, which measure 110 millimeters in diameter.

Trap shooting began as a competitive sport. It dates back to the 1830s and involved the shooting of live pigeons. Just what you wanted to learn, right? The birds in trap shooting all leave from the same area, flying away from the shooter. The barrels are longer on a trap shotgun and designed to shoot high. As with skeet, the ammunition utilized is lighter in recoil than most realize. Birdshot or skeet loads do not *recoil* or kick as much as the shot of a police load of .00 buckshot.

I call sporting clays *golf with a shotgun*. There is usually a sporting clays course at the same place where you shoot shotguns at trap and skeet. The courses are more elaborate than skeet or trap. They are both complex and expensive to establish. A sporting clay course is designed so each firing point simulates a specific species of game. A short walk from one point to another may provide pass shooting at ducks, flushing pheasants, or rabbits breaking from cover. In sporting clays, a round is usually considered to be fifty or one hundred targets, which are shot at five or ten stations, depending on the particular course. Unlike skeet, where the targets always fly the same path from each of two launchers, or trap, where the targets always fly within rigidly established limits as they rise and go away from the shooter, sporting clays involves the shooting of targets which can come from anywhere and fly in any direction relative to the shooter. This includes rabbit targets that bounce along the ground. Add to this that most sporting clay facilities change the courses regularly, and there is no way a shooter can get used to a particular method of shooting, as in trap and skeet. Guns for this even must be versatile and shoot accurately. They must be true to their point of aim, swing and point well. The balance of the gun must be neutral or the barrel slightly heavy to be most effective. Barrel lengths vary from shooter to shooter, but the most common is a 32 inch barrel with a universal choke, though anywhere from 26 inches to 34 inches should work. The longer dimensions are usually reserved for the experts.

If you wonder how it would be to be a Marine sniper, long distance rifle shooting may be for you. Competitive rifle shooting takes many forms: from the thousand yard course at Camp Perry to fifty foot basement ranges; from the ski-clothed shooters of biathlon competition to offhand wizards of high-powered silhouette shooting.

Camp Perry holds the national matches, which have been a proud tradition since 1907. Civilians shoot military-style rifles originally utilized for national defense. The weapons are extremely high grade, ranging from .22-caliber to 7-mm.

Another event, which is of a different challenge, is called the *Keneyathlon*. The Keneyathlon is a competition designed to separate the rifleman from the men with rifles. *Keneyous* is the Greek word for hunter, and *athlon* means test; thus, the Keneyathlon is the hunter's test. It is freestyle riflery. The targets are neither in plain sight nor at known distances. The shooters must judge for themselves the effects of the wind, distances, and the effective trajectory of the bullet. This sport also promotes the cardinal rule of shooting any weapon: unless you can guarantee the shot—unless you are willing to bet your house, family members, and dog on it—don't shoot. A wounded animal is a disgrace to hunters and an abomination in the eyes of the Creator. Knowing when to shoot is one of the greatest of hunting skills.

Bench-rest shooting is the art of shooting from a fixed point—a bench or tripod— where the object is to attain the perfect combination of rifle, load, and shooter. The shots must be so close together that they only make one hole in the paper. Formal Bench-rest competition got its start in the mid-1940s with an organization that went by the name of the Puget Sound Snipers Congress of Seattle, Washington. In the early days of competition, hunting and military rifles were used in a variety of homemade rests.

Today, bench-rest shooters use customized firearms that barely resemble rifles. They are designed to eliminate every human factor except wind calculation. The object is to shoot the tightest groups at distances of one hundred to three hundred yards. To do this, ammunition is hand-loaded to ridiculously accurate specifications. Bench-rest shooting is the art of sniping, without the victim.

Of course, I've but scratched the surface of all the events possible in the world of shooting sports, but I hope you get the picture that more is going on than you know about. I didn't even mention cowboy action shooting, shooting machine guns, silenced arms, the steel challenge, the International Defensive Pistol Association, or a bucket-load of other events, competitions, and disciplines I could write about.

CHAPTER 12

The Epistles

To My Sisters:

AFRICAN AMERICAN WOMAN, YOU alone have been responsible for the survival of our race. Your intelligence, will power, and inner strengths have been underestimated by all who have enslaved or sought to destroy our people. Because of this, you have been able to protect your children, shield them from life's atrocities, and teach us all to spiritually survive.

Even now, there are those who still seek to weaken, control, and destroy your children. Guns have been falsely blamed as the root of all evil. The word "gun" is an emotional hot button that evokes an emotional response and awakens your maternal instincts to once again save your people. In street terms, you are being played. I appeal to your intelligence to learn all you can about the issue of firearms.

Just like card sharks with a new poker player, savvy politicians and groups who understand what makes you spiritually unique are manipulating you. Without the facts, however, you will unknowingly contribute for the first time to the destruction of our people. You have been the secret weapon in the gun control battle for years. African American women unknowingly have been involved in the gun control struggle since the 1700's. When the black family was destroyed and made into chattel, it was the matriarch who remained. It was the woman who fed white and black children, cleaned their homes, and was used to keep her people in line. She is used even today to disarm the black community.

I have been to legislative hearings where grieving mothers who had lost their sons in drive-by shootings, gang and drug wars, being prostituted for their tears. Wearing the photos of their teenage and adult sons on pink tee shirts they, like other victims of violent crime, are used as poster children to forward the political careers of others. Your strong maternal instincts have gotten us through war, famine, disease, and slavery, but proof that you have been targeted for manipulation is that gun control groups use your tears and your suffering as sound bites in commercials and in public hearings.

As the unofficial leaders in our homes, teach your sons and daughters about safety and the reality of firearms. As grandmothers, remind your families about the struggles many of our people have forgotten.

The violence in our communities is a result of poverty, unemployment, drug and alcohol abuse, and the loss of the tight family structure. Aside from educating your children, you are going to have to learn to survive in a time when crime is out of hand. You have become the target of criminal predators and do not deserve to be a victim. Though our young people are using guns as the tools of their destruction, firearms are necessary tools. You are being used to disarm African Americans by allowing the increase of senseless and repetitive laws. By doing so, you allow the government through slicker means to accomplish something they have been trying to do since they brought our ancestors here in chains in the 1600s.

If the word "gun" evokes an emotional response in you and you don't really know why, think about changing that. Training saves lives. Education got our children off the plantation. You are still the hope of our people.

Sisters, take us forward, not backwards.

> *"You do not drown by falling in water; you only drown if you stay there."*

To My Brothers:

If you are an educated, conscious, or enlightened brother, you are probably already a gun owner.

Most black people readily associate guns exclusively with violent crimes, the plagues of terrorism, war, tragedy, and mayhem. Newspapers like *The Washington Post* and public officials make it seem that guns are the main problem of our society, but there are many cases that are not televised or reported where a gun has saved the owner from harm. If you protect yourself in this country, you are a vigilante, yet we are the only ones buying into this. White America hasn't stopped going to the pistol range and associating guns with wholesome recreation and security from crime and political tyranny. We, on the other hand, continue to believe what we are told. In order to take you into new territory, I have to show you where we have been.

The plight of African Americans today must partly be blamed on our short-term memory. We conveniently forget

122

that we were not always slaves. We conveniently forget that European scholars wrote the historical accounts we take as gospel.

The Wild West, for example, was full of African Americans and Native Americans who carried guns. Our roots are full of sharp-shooters, cowboys, and outlaws. Check out the history of pioneers like Mary Fields, Clara Brown, the Buffalo Soldiers, Ben Hodges, Cherokee Bill, the Deacons of Defense and Justice, and the Black Panther Party for Self-Defense. After you do, it will seem as if everyone from Great-Granddad to Aunt Minnie owned a gun. Those guns did not kill children. These men and woman, though newly emancipated, were more free in spirit than many of us today. They fought for knowledge, rights, and survival. That is what has kept me here in this space. Gun rights are civil rights. Yes, they are. Civil rights are the personal liberties that belong to an individual, owing to his or her status as a citizen or resident of a particular country or community. What makes us uniquely American is that we have The Bill of Rights, not a Bill of Needs. It is the first ten amendments to the U.S. Constitution. What it does is delineate our specific rights that are reserved for U.S. citizens and residents. Despite the crap you hear, no individual state (NY, IL, CO, CA, MD, DC) can remove or abridge rights that are guaranteed by the Constitution.

What rights are you fighting for today? Have you just sat on your laurels and sucked up all the benefits and not given back to the ancestors who died to get you where you are today? And if you haven't done anything, why get upset when a white dude, who just happens to be Ted Nugent, the 70's rocker turned gun rights activist and board member of the NRA, equates gun control with segregation and Jim Crow laws?

It's a people thing, I know. Just as when some Christians think that Catholics aren't going to heaven. Everybody wants to be right. The Bible even says that in the Old Testament book of Judges 21:25. Folks are still looking for a king.

("In those days there was no king in Israel; everyone did what was right in his own eyes." Judges 21:25)

Are you really angry that the white brother with the cowboy hat might be right? Civil rights are human rights. They are not just for black people. I know the Civil Rights Era is a sacred time period in our history and culture in America, but if you are truly free, if you are truly American, then color and who said it doesn't matter. What matters is the "content of our character." Am I wrong?

This brings us to the modern day panic over gun control. This issue is glossed over with so much sugar it will give you diabetes. This isn't the first time in history that the government has suggested we give up our guns to help fix the ills of society.

I'm here to tell you that guns are not evil. They are only mechanical devices, tools. True, they are on our streets in the hands of criminals, and brothers who are trapped in the criminal justice system trying to survive because they have no hope, but guns are not more evil than the money we all want to carry. A minister once told me money is not the root of all evil. He said that the *love of money* is what is evil. This statement is also true about firearms. People would prefer to blame the instruments of crime instead of focusing on the individuals responsible for the crime.

Today, the leading cause of death for Americans is ignorance. There are no statistics for that. What we don't know about parenting, finances, AIDS, guns, and the law is killing us. There are no quick fixes. Don't let the tears of your mother be used as propaganda against your rights. When you, the responsible, law- abiding brother, hear that you should turn in your guns, don't *buy* into it. That message is for the kids on the street, the stupid, and the criminals who shouldn't have guns anyway.

All efforts to repress and control our people throughout the centuries have been forced by racist, religious, and elitist beliefs. Many of the weapons on the market today, such as the street sweeper-type shotgun, the British Enfield rifle, and others, were originally designed specifically to kill Africans in South Africa. Gun control is racist. The strictest gun laws are in cities that have the highest concentrations of people of color. It is only about control. Of course, while many gun control advocates will state that these new laws are for the safety of everyone, the restrictions affect only a particular class of people.

If a European American shows up with a gun, our warped minds give him permission. He must legit, right? Until recently, with latest school and mall shootings, you would be ready to call him a cowboy, a police officer, or assume he was a soldier, wouldn't you? The reverse is unbelievable. A black man with a gun is still a negative image. And some knuckleheads relish it. The dreaded gangster rap image is big business. Is this a conspiracy? No. "It's nothing personal: it's just business."

The only people who don't have legally owned firearms in their homes are the African American citizens. This is proof positive that we have bought the lie, hook, line, and sinker. The people who want us unarmed and helpless don't have a hard time convincing us. They utilize the magazines our mothers read. Their media attack capitalizes on the fears and protective instincts of our black women.

In no time, they have disarmed Black America. They have successfully caused us to believe it is wrong to own a gun and to alienate our children, to sell them out as a lost generation, to abort them, or afterwards encouraged us to administer mind-controlling drugs to them. Worst of all, we have young men looking forward to going to prison as if it were the University of African America.

Don't embrace the anti-gun rhetoric that is written in *Ann Landers* columns and *The Washington Post* and shown on television. Racially motivated violence is not the only threat to which blacks are more vulnerable. An African American has at least a forty percent greater chance of being burgled and a one hundred percent greater chance of being robbed than a white person; we are exposed to more crime and are given less protection by the police. So that awful gun that is so politically incorrect today could probably save the life of your family or yourself. Don't wait for the police; they don't have to protect you.

Only free men carry guns; slaves cannot. Here is the first gun control law in Maryland:

1715. APRIL I GEORGE I, XXXII.

AND BE IT ENACTED, by the authority, advice and consent aforesaid, That no Negro or other slave within 'tis province shall be permitted to carry any gun, or, any other, offensive weapon, from off their masters land, without license from their said master; and if any Negro or other slave shall presume to do so, he shall be liable to be carried before a justice of peace, and be whipped, and his gun or other offensive weapon shall be forfeited to him that shall seize the same and carry such Negro so offending before a justice of peace.

To My Gay Friends:

I have come a long way from where I started twenty years ago in the gun rights movement. I have since learned that the Gay, Lesbian, Bi, Transgender (GLBT) group is another minority in America that is persecuted, assaulted, and murdered for being different. (I have just learned that if I were really hip I would say GLBTIQ, but I don't even know what those last two groups are.) All I know is that you guys really are different. You celebrate it. I am not a gay rights activist, but through this journey I have met and befriended a couple of folks (probably more than I know) who are a part of the gun community. It is from that standpoint and base that I implore you to consider arming yourself. Seek training and find out what firearms system works best for you. Since I started there is a new group of shooters called the Pink Pistols. Seek out a chapter rep in your area and get involved.

How did I get here? I defend everyone's right to keep and bear arms and to live free. To some people it's a no-brainer, but not so with my generation. It was one of those "aha moments" when I realized that African Americans weren't the only group which has been marginalized and attacked in a way that is socially acceptable. Can you believe it is socially acceptable to harm some groups and not others? All life is sacred. All people are equal. There is but one race, and that is the human one, but yet we categorize and give a higher preference to some over others. It is through this gun control argument that I learned about this and how other people really become better people by having to fight together. The Bible says that a *brother is born in adversity*. I understand that more and more as Americans who believe in the Second Amendment band together to fight those who don't. Those allies come in all forms, and it is amazing.

I learned that members of the "gay community" are often a silent group when it comes to crimes against them. Stuff you hear, the rest of us do not. And the truth is, we seldom care. When there is an assault against someone from the GLBT community and we are not a part of that, nobody talks about it.

I realized that you folks are living with some horrendous statistics of violence against you. So I advocate that you learn how to defend yourself with a gun. I advocate that you seek to carry concealed if your state allows for it. It is a high probability that if you live in a big city, you will be prohibited from doing so. And you are just another group being forsaken in America for whom we need change.

My awakening happened around 1998, while I was being interviewed by *The Baltimore Sun* newspaper with a man with long blonde hair, a bushy mustache, and a knee-length skirt. I thought as an activist this guy was more hardcore than I was. I thought it took some major courage to stand beside me on live TV wearing a dress and high heels. I thought maybe he was one of those diehard Redskin fans who wore the women's' outfits and the hog noses. I never got that tradition.

Believe it or not, my brother in arms was from the GLBT community. Call me slow, but I didn't know. He called me later and thanked me for being considerate of this transition. This was my first transgendered friend. He told me that he had to dress as a woman for a while before a psychologist would okay his paperwork to get physically altered/sex changed.

Okay! That was a bit much for this former Marine, because I thought I had heard everything. Obviously I had not. This was way outside my comfort zone. Before this conversation I was not the compassionate, understanding, nice guy he thought I was. I was the guy who laughed at gay jokes. I was the guy who gave thumbs up when he heard his friends had rolled a "fag" at the local bar. But here I was having a conversation with a fellow gun activist pouring out his guts to me. What I heard was tragic. He shared his pain growing up. He told me about his suicide attempts. Damn, he had some crappy stuff happen to him. I felt like the Grinch, (from the Dr. Seuss's Christmas poem), discovering I had a heart.

That was how it began. That was my entree into the world of another minority group in America outside my own. Sorry, I am slow.

One of the funny things I have noticed over the years is that even though almost all gun rights activists agree with me, we are still pretty conservative as a whole. When I had a member of the Pink Pistols, a gay gun group, on my podcast, *The Urban Shooter*, not a lot of comment or feedback followed socially. If I could input the sound of crickets right here, I would. And the same thing happens when an outspoken transgendered person who frequents the annual gun rights events sees me. She can clear a room.

If I can help you find an instructor or training, let me know. I am still not THAT progressive, but I respect you as another traveler in this world. I'll defend your right to be free.

CHAPTER 13

Violence

BY THE TIME YOU FINISH READING
this sentence a violent crime has occurred somewhere or reporting about it is being sold to the
media.

Unless it happened to you, before the Internet you didn't
read or hear about it as often, and we weren't able to tally up
the events as fast. Humanity has changed. We used to read
about all of the evils men do from the Department of Justice
Uniform Crime Report once a year (if it was prepared) for
statistics. Now all you have to do is set your browser to pull
up all the mayhem, daily. As a people we have a morbid fas-
cination with crime. Look at what we watch on television.

As a result, there is money to be made in carrying stories
that scare us. Our society is violence-loving. Our children
are dulled by it, accepting of it, and apathetic to most of it.
As a culture, I believe we have lost our morality. Everything

is permitted, and we can't determine what is foul. We care more for our pets than for our children. We care more about our appearances and food than we do our overall good.

If you wear a fur coat, you run the risk of having a rabid PETA (People for The Ethical Treatment of Animals) advocate throw paint on you (a dumb move). If you keep a dog chained up and isolated in your backyard for an extended period you can be fined and jailed for animal cruelty. Both of these crimes will evoke the ire of thousands of animal lovers. But if a person leaves a child alone in almost the same situation for an extended time in pursuit of their unfulfilled dreams, job fulfillment, travel, or something else, few eyebrows are raised. I don't think the same compassion for human life exists anymore. When that child becomes like an unsocialized dog, a sociopath, and/or a menace to society, we are quick to blame everything under the sun for the problem except the lack of parenting. If it really takes a village to raise a child, we are in trouble. Most children don't have a village or, at the least, a stable home.

Common sense is not as common as it used to be.

We believe most of what is printed or endorsed by celebrities, no matter how dumb it is. We want instant results, faster food, and less wait-time on everything. We love to adopt a hopeless solution if it sounds good. This is evident in the prevalence of the term "gun violence" and the frenzy it articulates.

"Gun violence" is a made-up term. There is just violence. Analytically, the term "gun violence" really means guns are perpetrating violence on other guns. You have to admit the term sounds good, though. It is a successfully-used emotional hot button for anyone who is or has been a victim. It also sounds good to anyone trying to persuade you into buying something. But we don't want to deal with reality. We have a problem with respect of life, liberty, and the pursuit of happiness. We have a problem with equality and justice. We have a problem with education and communication.

People kill with vehicles, garden tools, kitchen utensils, and everything possible, but it doesn't evoke the same response as the word "gun." We don't appreciate life as much as we should. Nor do we think much of ourselves and how ignorant we sound when we parrot incorrect statistics and sound bites or get enraged by the skillful manipulation of video or words. We have become weaker, easier to extort, and even easier to control.

Some version of a gun has been around since the Chinese invented gunpowder. Can you see how far we have come? Crime happens now because we have changed. Few of us have noticed. I can get elected, increase my ratings, make money on your response to fear and loss, all in the name of gun violence.

The emperor has no clothes.

Guns are erroneously blamed for violence. I say that boldly because violence occurs without the presence of a firearm. Having a gun in your vicinity does not embody you with demonic, murderous spirits. In communities with Central and South American, Southeast Asian, and some African ethnicities, violence and crimes of passion are often done with edged weapons instead of firearms.

How can we stop the violence in our society? What can we do to repair our communities without giving up the essential liberties that made this a great nation? What are you willing to do to protect your family from violence? What are you working in to make that a reality? Can we stop violence?

Children and the elderly have become the targets of everything wicked. Why? Because their innocence offends the very nature of the world today.

It's just so easy to blame a gun for the senseless murders of our loved ones and the innocent. It's so easy that everyone who doesn't legally own a gun does it. Guns do not equal violence. Having a firearm doesn't instantly make you a murderer, sociopath, or accident waiting to happen. What it does, unfortunately, is let demagogues turn on you for owning one to protect yourself or family, shoot recreationally, collect, or use to compete with. Gun stores this year are being assaulted for doing what they are in business to do, sell guns. I doubt if the Toyota dealer will be protested by Rev. Jesse Jackson for the hit and run the driver of the Toyota caused or the liquor store shut down for the booze that impaired the man down the street so badly that he no longer has the decency not to hurt his wife. We have more than a few problems in our society. One of them is a loss of respect for life and a penchant for all things easy.

Do you know how hard it is for a person to legally get a firearm? And do you know how hard it is for a person to get a permit, permission, and zoning to be able to legally sell them? Every state is different. Urban areas are extremely tough. And all the gun laws already on the books still don't deter criminals, since by definition they do not obey the law. Don't believe the hype put out by politicians who are riding this issue for fame and glory. Criminals spend all of their mental energy on how to usurp the law.

You have no idea how much you don't know! If politicians and anti-gun groups really wanted to help the communities, they would provide training and education for everyone, budget more money for policing, prosecute every gun crime, refuse plea-bargains, and insist on mandatory sentences for crimes where a firearm was used.

CHAPTER 14

The Police

ONE OF THE ARGUMENTS FOR GUN control is that the police are there to protect us. The truth is, they are not. The truth is, their sidearm is for their personal protection, not yours.

If the police got themselves together, or the government created a better police force, would the gun argument fade away?

No. I believe the majority of the men and women you see in law enforcement are doing a great job. They are doing the very best they can with the budget, resources, training, and strength they have available. It takes a lot of mental discipline to do what they do every day. They see us at our worst. When we are speaking to them it is rarely friendly. It is rarely to seek their concerns. We want something. We need something. Something has gone wrong and we want someone to fix it. We don't know if they can or not, but we do know that since they wear a uniform and a badge that denote they are representatives of the "authorities," then maybe they have a better chance at it that we do.

Police officers are not paid a lot of money. They do it out of love for the job, people, and justice. They work long hours and brave the environment. They deal with being unpopular while at the same time needed. They grow cynical and have a unique sense of humor because they see all kinds of people every day and night.

We forget that police officers are human. Yes, they are professionals; but they want to go home after every shift, and so they pick and choose their battles. Being human, police officers come with all the prejudices, ailments, and shortcomings the rest of us have. When you call on them in the dead of night because you hear strange sounds in your house, understand that the person coming to respond may have worked a double shift. He or she may never have dealt with a person of your race, gender, ethnic background, or sexual preference. A law enforcement officer who arrives late at night might not show you all the professional courtesies he or she is supposed to.

Believe it or not, safeguarding your life, your property, and your family is your responsibility.

Most of us want to believe we live in a society where the police are perfect and criminals fear them. Most people want to believe in something. Try Jesus. Everything else will let you down. We are so desperate to believe that we are duped. Police and politicians have no legal duty to protect you. State and city governments, rather than the federal authorities, are responsible for local law enforcement, so only occasionally have federal courts ruled on the matter of police protection.

The US Supreme Court declared in 1856 that the local law enforcement had no duty to protect a particular person, and only a general duty to enforce the laws.

The Fourteenth Amendment to the U.S. Constitution gives you no right to police protection. In 1982, the Seventh Circuit Court of Appeals held that:

> *"There is no constitutional right to be protected by the state against being murdered by criminals or madmen. It is monstrous if the state fails to protect its residents against such predators but it does not violate the due process clause of the Fourteenth amendment or, we suppose, any other provision of the Constitution. The Constitution is a charter of negative liberties: it tells the state to let people alone; it does not require the federal government or the state to provide services, even so elementary a service as maintaining law and order."*

There are few exceptions to rulings of this nature. In 1983, the District of Columbia Court of Appeals remarked that:

> *"In a civilized society, every citizen at least tacitly relies upon the constable for protection from crime. Hence, more than general reliance is needed to require the police to act on behalf of a particular individual. Liability is established, therefore, if the police have specifically undertaken to protect a particular individual and the individual has specifically relied upon the undertaking. Absent a special relationship, therefore, the police may not be held liable for the failure to protect a particular individual from harm caused by criminal conduct. A special relationship exists if the police employ an individual in aid of law enforcement, but does not exist merely because an individual requests or a police officer promises to provide protection."*

As a result, our government – specifically, the police – has no legal duty to help any given person, even one whose life is in imminent danger. The only exceptions would be for a person who can prove he or she has helped the police force as an informant, as a witness, or in some similar capacity.

On March 16, 1975, Washington, DC resident Carolyn Warren called the police about two intruders who had smashed the back door to her house and attacked a female housemate. After calling the police, Warren and another housemate took refuge on a lower back roof of the building. The police went to the front door and knocked. Warren, afraid to go downstairs, could not answer. The police officers left without checking the back door.

Warren again called the police and was told they would respond. Assuming they had returned, Warren called out to the housemate, thus revealing her location. The two intruders then rounded up all three women. For the next fourteen hours the women were held captive, raped, robbed, beaten, forced to commit sexual acts upon each other, and made to submit to the sexual demands of the intruders. A police cruiser circled the home without stopping, and another officer knocked on the door but left when no one answered. Of course these women tried to sue the District of Columbia government for negligence.

In the case, a lower court upheld the women's claim, saying, "When a police department employee tells frantic callers that help is on the way, it is reasonably foreseeable that the person so assured may forego, to their detriment, other avenues of help."

But the decision was overturned by the DC Court of Appeals, which said the dispatcher's assurances were not sufficient to overcome the general barrier to suits against police and that the department's obligation was only to the general public, not to particular individuals. The Superior Court of the District of Columbia held that:

> *"The fundamental principal is that a govern-*
> *ment and its agents are not under general duty*
> *to provide public services, such as police pro-*
> *tection, to any particular individual citizen. The*
> *duty to provide public services is owed to the*
> *public at large, and, absent a special relation-*
> *ship between the police and an individual, no*
> *specific legal duty exists."*

In an accompanying memorandum, the court explained that the term "special relationship" did not mean an oral promise to respond to a call for help. Rather, it involved the provision of help to the police force.

Even someone repeatedly threatened by another is not entitled to police protection until having been physically harmed. Back in 1959, an ex-boyfriend who had a criminal record terrorized New Yorker Linda Riss. Over several months, he repeatedly threatened her, saying things like, "If I can't have you, no one else will have you," and "When I get through with you, no one else will want you." She repeatedly sought police protection, explaining her request in detail. Nothing was done to help her. When he threatened her with immediate attack, she again urgently begged the New York City Police Department for help but was again refused. The next day, she was attacked; a thug hired by her persecutor threw sodium hydroxide in her face. She was blinded in one eye and her face permanently scarred.

The Court of Appeals of New York ruled that Linda Riss had no right to protection. Further, the court refused to create such a right because that would impose a crushing economic burden on the government, ruling that only the legislature could create a right to protection.

The resources of the community limit the amount of protection that may be provided and require a considered legislative executive decision as to how these resources may be deployed. For the courts to proclaim a new and general duty of protection, even to those who may be the particular seekers of protection based on specific hazards, could and would inevitably determine how the limited police resources of the community should be allocated, and without predictable limits.

Judge Keating dissented, bitterly noting that Linda Riss was victimized not only because she had relied on the police to protect her, but also because she obeyed the New York laws that forbade her to own a weapon. He wrote:

> *"What makes the city's position particularly difficult to understand is that, in conformity to the dictates of the law, Linda did not carry any weapon for self-defense. Thus, by a rather bitter irony she was required to rely for protection on the City of New York, which now denies all responsibility to her."*

In the West, the New Mexico Court of Appeals ruled that the Bernalillo County Sheriff's Department could not be held liable for failing to protect a woman who was being raped and tortured, even though deputies were notified that the attack was in progress. In this case, Schear v. Board of County Commissioners of Bernalillo et al., the three-judge panel unanimously said law officers have a duty only to the general public, not to specific individuals who are attacked by criminals.

According to the suit, the plaintiff was brutally raped and tortured in her home on February 6, 1982. Before the attacks, the Bernalillo County Sheriff's Office received an emergency telephone call from Anthony Pena, who stated that an armed perpetrator had broken into the woman's house, assaulted Pena with a shotgun, and forced him out of the building. The sole response of the sheriff's office was to dial the woman's telephone number; but there was no response, because the assailant would not allow the woman to answer the phone. Pena called the police again but was informed that the department had decided to take no further action in response to the calls.

The woman sued the department, claiming the Sheriff's office was negligent in not responding to criminal acts and in failing to investigate the incident, but the case was dismissed by District Court Judge Thomas J. Mescall. Writing for the appeals court, Judge William Bivins said that a citizen's request for aid did not create a special duty under which police must provide assistance. Bivins called the attitude of the Sheriff's department "lackadaisical" and "cavalier" but cited the 1968 case of Riss v. City of New York that held:

> *"To foist the presumed cure for these [criminal attack] problems by judicial innovations of a new kind of liability in tort would be foolhardy indeed and an assumption of judicial wisdom and power not possessed by the courts."*

The New Mexico decision joins a growing body of case law that grants police and other government bodies immunity from negligence suits. The bottom line is that your life is in your own hands. There are now many cases clearly showing that under U.S. law:

† No individual has a right to police protection, even when life is in clear and immediate peril.

† There is no right to police protection, simply because there are not enough police resources available to enable every person who feels threatened to be protected.

✝ To make police officers answerable to individual citizens for failure to provide protection would make police officers afraid to do anything for fear that an action or inaction would expose them to civil liability.

Now that I've thoroughly depressed you, I'll give you some hope. The Second Amendment was provided in the Constitution specifically for law-abiding citizens to protect themselves from tyranny and criminal acts. The writers of the Constitution knew that we are ultimately responsible for our own personal safety. So before someone tries to amend a ratified part of the Bill of Rights, i.e., the Second Amendment, thinking it is an old and arbitrary document, stand up for it!

The real problem is that we have lost faith in just about everything. We mix our arguments with the police with our mistrust of the justice system, the executive branch and the legislative branches of the government.

There is an industry of incarceration.

We want more government services but don't know what we are asking for when we do.

We have lost real family values. We have lost faith in God. We have lost faith in our education system.

The enemy is fear. We think it is hate; but, it is fear.

---Gandhi

CHAPTER 15

Your First Gun

WHEN YOU MAKE THE DECISION to legally buy and or carry a gun, you are on your own. You will not be politically correct or very popular for your decision. The question of firearm ownership is personal. It is a choice that should be made by you, the individual, not your friends or the government. It should be made with the head, not the heart.

The number one reason for buying a firearm is for self-defense. Secondary is for fun. Are you tired of being associated with victims? I wrote the first edition of this book part time in a small room of a metropolitan church because I was tired of hearing the lies that are told so many times that if I didn't know better, I'd believe them, too. I was tired of having my people slaughtered, abused, neglected, and lied to about guns. As a firearms instructor, as a grown man who was raised in a home with a loaded shotgun leaning against the wall, I know that having a gun in the house does not increase your risk of suicide. That is the kind of stuff you hear when you are considering becoming a gun owner. Suicide is a serious problem. It is a sickness. It is the loss of hope. It has nothing to do with gun ownership. If someone has a mental problem they will still have it with or without a gun in the house.

Folks love statistics, so I'll give you a few to keep people off your back. I won't debate statistics with anyone. Statisticians can make any point with any set of numbers. Here are some you never hear:

- † 99.8% of all guns owned in America are not used in crimes.
- † Guns are used four times as often in self-defense as in crime and 98% of the time, not even fired.
- † Only 1% of the time when a gun is being used in defense does the criminal take the gun from the defender.
- † After guns were banned in England, the armed robbery rate spiked over 40%, and 44% in Australia.
- † Only 4% of guns used in crimes were obtained legally.

So what do you buy?

Four factors should influence your decision. The firearm's use, cost, quality, and fit. Sounds like a pair of shoes or a hand tool, right? Well that is exactly what firearms are: tools. Some use them for recreation, some for show, and some for protection. What are you going to use your gun for? Your choices could be a gun for sport, self-defense, home protection, hunting, to collect, or any combination of these. How much cash are you willing to put out for your first purchase? Bear in mind that cost does not always equal quality.

Go to a public target range and try shooting a number of different guns with an instructor or someone knowledgeable about gun safety and range etiquette so you can see firsthand which one is for you. Don't let the gun store clerk, the military veteran, or your Uncle Bob sell you a gun you haven't personally investigated. The gun itself could be a technological wonder; but if it doesn't fit your body and its needs, it is not for you.

What level of quality do you want or need from your gun purchase? The longer you are expecting to keep your gun, the higher quality you should seek. The more pride in ownership you anticipate, the more value you should place on your gun. For example, if you are looking for a standard twelve-gauge shotgun for home protection that you never expect to fire, the lower-priced shotguns will give you the best value. A very detailed, semiautomatic trap gun that will be shot often would likely cost a little more and should not be the one you get. Therefore, you should be willing to fork out the bucks for more service before and after the sale. A further consideration is that guns made from stamped metal parts are usually cheaper than those which are hand-tooled. There are examples of these less expensive types around. One brand comes to mind that comes from Highpoint, NC. This brand has gotten better and all but the gun snobs seem to be happy with their cost point and use. Hand-tooled pistols, made within certain specifications, are more accurate; hence the higher price tag. Heckler and Koch and Sig-Sauer pistols are good examples of high quality, high-priced arms. Glock pistols are an exception, because they are made from less expensive materials but are very high in quality. And that was me trying to be helpful without trying to sound like a commercial for Glock, which I love. Glock pistols are a great buy because they are reliable, and like a good watch. The downside is that they are striker fire pistols, without a traditional safety, (although they have three safeties), and require training to be used effectively.

All guns are not created equal. When you chose one, how does the gun feel to you? This final consideration involves the ergonomics of the weapon. Every rifle and every handgun should fit the user. Shotguns can be fitted with shorter stocks, butt plates, pistol grips, and longer barrels, if need be. Pistols can be fitted with taller and larger sights, fingered, fatter, slimmer, shorter, and longer grips. After you find the caliber you want to use, compose a gun for your comfort. A gun that fits adds to your accuracy and enjoyment. Smith and Wesson has created an M&P series that people rave over. Glock has new interchangeable grips and everybody makes smaller pistols now. Try before you buy. The grip of a 9-mm Browning High-Power may feel better than the grip of a Sig-Sauer P-226 9-mm. A shotgun or rifle that fits is one you can place into a shooting position easily, smoothly, and gracefully. The butt cradles into your shoulder almost automatically your cheek settles on the stock naturally, and your dominant eye looks out over the barrel without undue strain or awkward head tilting. Your trigger finger slips into the trigger guard easily without reaching. Remember that guns can be made to fit your body type and that certain guns are more user-friendly than others are, so compare firearms before choosing one.

There are three primary ways to buy a new firearm legally. You can obtain one from a Federal Firearms Licensee (FFL), at gun shows, or at a store that has the license to sell. In some states you are able to buy used guns from friends or family who reside in the same state as you, but gun laws are changing annually. This is one of the so-called "loop-holes" that doesn't exist. Do an online search with your state of record (where you have your driver's license and vote); ask the local gun shop for the latest laws. They know. Not doing so can make you an outlaw. used guns rarely are used as much as you think unless previously owned by a gun enthusiast, cop, military person, or competitive shooter. There is a blue book of wholesale values for new guns, but no really concrete prices exist for the sale of used ones. Your local FFL holder can order your gun and has the right to charge what he/she wants. This can save you a penny or two, but don't expect help after the sale. Gun shows are another alternative to the gun store and, depending on the state, you could walk out with the weapon on the same day. In some places you will have to comply with waiting periods before picking up your new firearm. Sometimes buying at a gun show is a hassle because, contrary to popular opinion, you can't always walk out with your new purchase. You have to travel to the store of the gun show salesman or have your gun sent to a shop in your area. You can only buy a gun in the state in which you reside. This is not a free service, however. The seller sends the gun and the store charges between ten and twenty dollars for the use of his FFL and his shop address. This process is often used when you wish to buy a gun in a state other than the one in which you live.

You can even get a gun online. Sounds scary, huh? The truth is, you can buy it from an online auction and the owner of the gun you buy has to ship it to an FFL dealer near you to handle the federal and state requirements. It won't come to your doorstep unless you have a hard-to-get FFL dealer's or curio's license.

There are many gun manufacturers, and guns come in all sizes, shapes, and prices. There are name brands, no-names, and, as in other markets, imitations. Depending on what you want, what your need is, and how much you can afford, there is a firearm for you. Some are more versatile than others. Some are single-purpose tools. Others can be used for more than one purpose.

Guns are designed for work, play, sale, and display. Since European Americans dominate the market in firearms at this time, advertising, construction, and development of firearms are configured toward them. Public opinion also tends to change gun design. Small, concealable weapons that were once affordable are not made known because of laws concerning "Saturday Night Specials." Quality didn't change on some pistols, just the price. When Glock first introduced their line of pistols, they were called the Plastic Guns. That was okay until plastic got a bad name. The media-believing populace thought plastic guns could be smuggled in airline luggage and onboard aircraft.

Manufacturers do cater to the machismo of their buyers. Here's an example: A new gun from a certain manufacturer has an extended trigger well. Suddenly, the next newly designed guns from other manufacturers all have the same feature. Why put it on the next generation of guns? It sells. A feature that was originally designed for cold weather use with a gloved hand is now a must-have item. Stereotypically, men like gadgets. If it squeaks, pops, blinks, shines, or gurgles, men have to have it. The gun industry is obliged to produce marketable products. Things like walnut or stag grips, lacquered stocks, trigger shoes, engraved slides and barrels, custom finishes, and anodized aluminum don't make a weapon any more accurate or make it operate more efficiently. But since men have to have these things, the gun industry supplies them. Some of it is just foolishness.

Free money-making tip: if you want to invent something and get rich, make it for a firearm. If it is a novelty, doesn't get anyone killed, and can be showcased by a TV or movie star on film, you're in. Think about the stars and their weapons for a moment. I guarantee that if you gave it some thought you could name and match the gun with the star. Remember the firearm Chuck Connors had in the western? What did

Dirty Harry carry? James Bond? What did George C. Scott carry in the movie *Patton*? Don Johnson in *Miami Vice*? If you can name any of those, do you see how Hollywood has influenced us? The same is happening today in video games.

Hollywood influences the gun world, and so does the law enforcement community. Most officers don't realize the hype to which they are subject and which they perpetuate. The Federal Bureau of Investigation, known to some as the authority in law enforcement knowledge, has a major impact on the rest of the country. After the infamous Miami incident of 1986, when two desperadoes held off a number of agents after being shot numerous times, everyone wanted bigger guns. They went back and forth between calibers. 9mm or 10mm? 10mm or .40 S&W? Or go back to the tried and true, circa 1911 .45 cal ACP? The nines didn't stop the bad guys all the time. The "tens" rattled the eyeballs of the FBI's weaker shooters and the frames of most autoloaders. They even tried to change the ammo. They wanted "man-stopper" rounds, ammunition that will cause a criminal to instantly cease from causing further harm. So ballistics wizards and alchemists tried hard to satisfy those needs, marketing rounds like the Hydro-shock, the Black Talon, silver tips, hollow points, and so forth, that fed upon the need but were not necessarily doing what they were supposed to.

So what is the answer? What kind of gun do you get? What kind of bullets do you need? To answer these questions fairly, you must add into the equation the purpose, the resources, the skill, and the knowledge of the shooter.

I am a firm believer that a well-placed round is all that counts; but in terms of simple protection, many things weigh into account when you are trying stop someone from causing further harm. The human body is a masterpiece of creation. If the mind doesn't want the body to stop, it won't. It can do superhuman things. The gun, the round, and the shooter must work together within their own limitations and those of the adversary.

Training will save you money and save your life. Seek some before you buy and you'll thank me. Firearm ownership is not for everyone, but it should be for anyone who has not given up his or her right to do so. Buying a firearm should be an educated decision, not an emotional one.

CHAPTER 17

Silencers

I TRY TO ATTEND THE SHOOTING, Hunting and Outdoor Trade Show every year now that I have a small media business. It gives me the opportunity to see new products and people in the firearms community whom I wouldn't normally see. One class of items I wasn't aware of but really like now is silencers or suppressors for firearms. Like many people, I didn't realize how cool having a silencer could be. The movies help us believe they are only for bad guys and assassins. The more enlightened among us may even think it's okay for Special Forces to have them to take out terrorists but see little application for the regular law-abiding gun enthusiast. I found out that "silencers," as they are classified by the Bureau of Alcohol, Tobacco, Firearms, and Explosives (BATFE), are legal to own, if you have the money and can pass the background check, which includes fingerprinting, photos, and a long wait.

To keep silencers out of the hands of bad guys after their invention in the Roaring Twenties, the U.S. government put a $200 tax on each one and a separate requirement for background checks like they do on handguns. The federal government created the National Firearms Act (NFA) in 1934; it is a list of arms like short-barreled rifles and shotguns (which are considered short if the barrel is under 18 inches), machine guns, and even devices like mortars, howitzers, and grenade launchers which are not allowed to be owned by private citizens.

A lot of well-meaning people don't know that you cannot go into a WalMart and walk out with a silencer or an NFA-listed weapon. If you are not a criminal, have the money to pay the excise tax per item, and don't mind going through a strict process, you can get a silencer.

I bet you wonder why anyone would want one, right?

The report from guns is naturally loud. It can damage your hearing. You need to take significant precautions to protect your hearing when shooting. Outdoor shooting ranges get closed down unfairly all the time because of the noise levels coming from ranges nearby after a slick developer puts houses on what was once rural or uninhabited land.

Silencers or suppressors, (the names are interchangeable, and both are correct), is a muffler screwed on or made onto the barrel of a firearm that quiets the thing. It's a good thing to have, because not only are you saving your hearing, but also you are being considerate of others.

If you want to buy one, no license is required. If you can legally purchase a handgun in your state and are over 21 years old you can get a silencer. You must pay the US Treasury a special $200 per firearm tax. You will probably have to have a Chief Law Enforcement Officer (CLEO) in your area sign off on your Form 4, (application to transfer a

NFA firearm), which you get when you buy the silencer. A background check is done; that will include two sets of FBI fingerprint cards, which will be mailed to the BATFE. The BATFE checks their databases to see if what you are purchasing is legal, transferrable, and owned by the FFL, and then you wait. I am told the wait is from six to twelve weeks, which to me means six months. Once you are approved, one of the Forms is returned and you can pick up your silencer. The same thing works for any NFA or Class III item.

CHAPTER 18

Last Shots

Gun control is not new. Race is still used today by all races of people to control and manipulate the uninitiated into voting and acting the way they want. I have discovered that there are people of all colors who mean us no good. I have learned that anybody who seeks to take away my right to live free, or to limit my freedom, thus guaranteed by the US Constitution and the Bill of Rights, is not my friend.

I choose to be a gun owner and don't force my choices on anyone. I defend my right not to be persecuted for that. I defend the rights my ancestors have died for. I defend the right of my descendants not yet born. Fighting for freedom has cost me a lot. Freedom isn't free.

Too many African Americans falsely believe that gun control works. The cities of New York, Washington, DC, Philadelphia, Los Angeles, Cincinnati, New Jersey, Baltimore, and parts of North Carolina have more restrictive gun laws than the rest of the entire country. Are you any safer because of it? The definition of insanity is to do the same thing repeatedly and expect a different result. When will we get it? When will we stop listening to the plantation mentality of the apathetic masses, the uninformed and those who don't mean us any good?

Have you noticed all the references to becoming ready for the next big emergency? Not since Y2K has there been such a push by the government to provide information about emergency preparedness. Are you ready for the next pandemic, terrorist attack, or natural disaster? This gun issue is not about duck hunters or old white guys with long guns. The Parker case is about self-reliance, personal protection, and you. It may be time to change your thinking and learn how to protect what's yours. Don't let politicians continue to speak erroneously and take away rights you were born with. You have the right to live without fear of losing your life.

Gun ownership does not equate to murder. Our ancestors brought military arms back from the wars they fought. Our brothers and uncles in law enforcement still own firearms. Despite the fact that shooting is a sport you may enjoy, firearms are tools you need to protect your family from predators. You don't have to be a victim.

I have learned from the gun community what is right in America. My brothers and sisters in arms are the kind of people who make me proud to be an American. Gun owners of all kinds have enriched my life with conversation, fun, fellowship, and good will. We have struggled through prohibition and bigotry together. We have struggled socially and culturally to learn what is acceptable and what is not. We have had awkward moments and "aha" ones. We have become family. We are as diverse as the shoes in my daughter's closet but belong to the same pair of legs called America, and she is still beautiful.

Shalom, baby!

About the Author:

Reverend Blanchard is internationally known as the Black Man With A Gun. (http://blackmanwithagun.com) He is a Christian evangelist, author, and gun rights activist with a background in counter-terrorism and police instruction. He is a former U.S. Marine, trained by Department of State and the Central Intelligence Agency (CIA). He speaks Brazilian Portuguese and has a working knowledge of Spanish.

He served as one of the first African-American members of the Director of Central Intelligence protective staff and firearms instructors. He has traveled to more than twelve countries in protection of CIA Directors Casey, Gates, and Webster, diplomats and officials.

He has served as a columnist for *New Voices Newspaper* of Durham, North Carolina; as a Director and Chaplain of the National Law Enforcement Group, the Law Enforcement Alliance of America. He has lobbied and testified before the United States Congress, Texas, South Carolina, Wisconsin, Michigan, Virginia, and Maryland for an individual's right to self-defense.

With two decades of gun rights activism, Blanchard has been involved in almost every pro-rights event that involved a person of color. He has done commercials for TV against racist gun laws and has been featured in four documentaries.

He produces a weekly podcast called *Black Man With A Gun Show*, now in its seventh year. It has received over 70 thousand downloads in one month. He is a sought-after speaker and sage in the gun community. He is a trusted source and advocate. He has a growing network of podcast and blogs found at http://blanchardmediagroup.com.

Appendix I - Terminology

The following pages contain terms used in the world of firearms. This is gun-speak. You cannot communicate with gun people without using these terms. Take a few moments to familiarize yourself with them. It will make easier your further reading in other books on the topic of guns.

Accurize: To modify, rework, and refine a weapon to improve the characteristics of the designed function and accuracy capabilities.

ACP: Automatic Colt Pistol cartridge.

Action: The part to which the barrel is attached. In a rifle it is often called the receiver. Shotgun or double-barreled sections house all the mechanisms or working parts. The term may be further modified as side-action, breech-action, belt-action, snap-action, etc. It is also used to indicate the different forms of charging the weapon as bolt-action, lever-action, pump-action, etc.

Adjustable trigger: One that can be adjusted for weight of pull.

Aperture sights: A front or rear sight, primarily for a rifle, with a circular opening in the center. Interchangeable discs with holes of varying diameters may be inserted to control the sight picture according to shooting conditions.

Auto-loading: A type of arm in which the force of the explosion of the first shot is used to unlock the mechanism, to extract or eject the empty shell, and to reload by stripping and feeding another cartridge from the magazine into the chamber. The trigger must be pressed for each successive shot.

Automatic: Arms in which the force of the explosion of the first shot is used to continue the operation of unlocking, extraction, ejection, reloading, locking, and firing continuously, as long as the ammunition lasts in the magazine, belt, or strip and the pressure on the trigger is continued. The name is commonly applied erroneously to auto-loading, repeating hand firearms.

Back strap: The rear extension of a pistol or revolver frame that curves downward between the grips.

Ball: Round lead ball used as a bullet in most muzzle-loading rifles and pistols.

Ball screw: Used in muzzle-loading, this looks like a wood screw. It threads into the end of the ramrod. It can be twisted into the soft lead ball when it is inside the barrel. Then the ball can be pulled backwards to unload the rifle when it has been fired.

B.A.R.: Abbreviation for Browning Automatic Rifle, a gas-operated military weapon invented by John M. Browning (1885-1926).

Barrel: Metal tube containing the chamber and bore of a firearm.

Barrel length: The distance between the muzzle and the rear face, breech, of the barrel where it abuts the breech bold or bolt, thus including the chamber. Revolver barrel lengths do not include the chamber, their chambers being in the cylinder. The design of a barrel length takes into account the burning rate of the propellant powder to be used and the projectile to be fired.

Barrel lug: A projection integral with the barrel, used to secure the magazine, forearm, or some moveable part to the barrel.

Bead: A small snob of metal on a firearm near the muzzle, used for a front sight in aiming.

Bench-rest: A specially constructed shooting bench at which the shooter sits to support his elbow and the gun barrel. Bench-rest shooting is concerned with firing groups as small as possible at a target over measured distances and with any type of rifle and cartridge best adapted for super-accurate performance.

Biathlon: An event combining a cross-country race on skis and firing a rifle at various distances. This was even included in the 1960 Olympic Winter Games.

Binocular vision: Sighting with both eyes open.

Bipod: A two-legged stand or mount; i.e., a stand for a spotting scope or the mount for a mortar or a long rifle.

Blow back: *(1)* Escape, to the rear and under pressure, of gases formed during the firing of the gun. May be caused by a defective breech mechanism, a ruptured cartridge or case, or a faulty primer. *(2)* Type of weapon operation in which the force of expanding gases acting to the rear against the face of the bolt furnishes all the energy required to initiate the complete cycle of operations of the gun. A weapon which employs this method of operation is characterized by the absence of any breech lock or bolt lock mechanism.

Blow forward: A type of automatic action in which the barrel is blown forward, then returns against the standing breech by spring pull, reloading taking place during the return movement.

Bluing: Purposely rusting metal by artificial oxidation to form a protective coating.

Bolt: A sliding mechanism that closes the breech in some types of extractors and firing pins and supports the base of the cartridge case.

Bolt action: A rifle and shotgun mechanism whereby the breech is opened and closed by a manually operated bolt which travels back and forth in the receiver in a direct line with chamber and barrel. *(1) Turning bolt*—locking lugs turned to lock the action. *(2) Straight pull*—locking lugs actuated by bolt studs, which slide in grooves cut into the bolt cylinder.

Bolt face: That portion of the bolt which engages and supports the head of the cartridge.

Bore: *(1)* The interior of the barrel through which the charge or bullet passes. *(2)* The diameter measured from land to land. (See **land**.)

Breech: The rear end of the barrel into which the cartridge is inserted.

Breech plug: Plug which screws into the rear end of a muzzle-loader's barrel. It seals the back end of the barrel.

Buckshot: Large-size lead balls (shot) for use in shotgun shells. Commercially manufactured in five sizes, with the following designations and diameters: No. 00(.33"); No. 0(.32"); No. 1(.30") and (.25"); No. 4(.24").

Bullet gauge: Gauges normally used to measure the diameter and concentricity of a bullet.

Butt: The shoulder end of a gun stock; the bottom of a revolver or pistol grip. Loosely used to indicate the complete butt-stock of rifles and shotguns or the grip of a handgun.

Butt plate: A metal, plastic, or rubber covering for the rear edges of a gunstock, usually corrugated to prevent slipping from the shoulder. On some rifles, butt plates are adjustable for vertical movement and may have extension prongs, which fit under and/or over the shoulder.

Caliber: Bore diameter of a rifle or handgun, measured from one land to the opposite land, or the diameter before rifling, designated in fractions of an inch or millimeters, although a stated caliber may not be an exact figure. Black powder calibers, such as .45-70-405, means .45"diameter, 70 as the weight of the powder charge, and 405 as the weight of the bullet in grams; many of these old designations were incorporated into modern smokeless powder nomenclature, but the second figure is meaningless. Designations such as .250-3000 refer to caliber and muzzle velocity; 8 mm. X 56 refers to caliber and length in millimeters.

Cam: A rotating or sliding projection that either imparts to or receives a motion from a counteracting part, such as roller, pin, etc. Thus, a *camming* action.

Centimeter Chamber: 1/100 of a meter, or 0.3937 inch.

Chamfer Charger: The compartment at the rear of a gun barrel that holds a charge or cartridge; one of the compartments in the cylinder of a revolver. Also, the action of inserting a round of ammunition into the chamber of a firearm. To bevel. Chamfering a cartridge case means beveling the inside of it by cutting or rolling the edge.

Choke: *(1)*Any container used in muzzle-end of a shotgun barrel that controls the shot pattern; the difference between bore and parallel diameters, expressed in thousandths of an inch, or points. The wider the pattern desired, the less the amount of choke required. Degree of choke is measured by approximate percentage of pellets striking within a 30" circle at forty yards. *(2)*Constriction at the muzzle-end of a shotgun barrel which controls the shot pattern; the difference between bore and parallel diameters, expressed in thousandths of an inch, or points. The wider the pattern desired, the less the amount of choke required. Degree of choke is measured by approximate percentage of pellets striking within a 30" circle at forty yards.

Chronograph: An electric or electronic device for recording a projectile's time of flight, from which velocities are computed.

Clip: (Most misused term in the shooting world-*authors note*). *(1)Cartridge clip*—open top and bottom metal container for cartridges that is pressed into the magazine well. Cartridges are fed from it into the chamber by the loading mechanism; automatic ejection of the clip follows feeding of the last cartridge. *(2) Mannlicher clip*—Mauser-type clip or charger is a metal band, which holds the cartridge for stripping into the magazine from the top by manual pressure. This type of clip does not remain in the magazine, but is either removed before firing or ejected by the closing of the bolt.

Cock: To draw the hammer or cocking-piece back into firing position either manually or by pressure on the trigger; also, to top-set the trigger for firing. In a half-cock position, the hammer or cocking-piece is partially retracted but mechanically prevented from contacting the firing pin.

Compensator: A device used on the barrel of a weapon to reduce recoil.

Cross bolt: A movable, locking bar at right angles to the bore, which either locks or strengthens the locking mechanism of a closed breech, usually that of a break-type shotgun. Some bolt-action guns may use a cross bolt to lock the bolt in an open position.

Cycle rate: The rate, at which a succession of movement

repeats itself, applied to rate of fire of an automatic weapon.

Cylinder: *(1)* True diameter of the bore of a shotgun barrel, hence without any degree of choke. Delivers a 25% to 35% shot charge pattern. (See **choke**.) *(2)*A round steel block, the inside of which is bored with multiple chambers for cartridges. Used as the loading device for revolvers; formerly in some types of rifles—notable Colt.

Decibel: A unit of measure used in evaluation of sound levels. Measurement is made by a sound level meter. Example: sound in a quiet business office is about forty decibels; average street traffic one hundred feet away is from sixty to seventy decibels; a gunshot registers about one hundred decibels; and a boiler shop is about one hundred and thirty decibels, just below the limit of endurance of the human ear.

Double action: That type of firing action whereby a single pull of the trigger both cocks and fires the weapon. It is employed in revolvers and old types of rifles and shotguns. It contrasts with single action, which requires the hammer to be cocked by hand prior to firing by pulling the trigger. (See **single action**.)

Dry fire: Practice with an unloaded weapon.

Ejection: The process by which a case or cartridge is thrown from the weapon by ejector. The process of removing a live or spent shell or cartridge case from the chamber.

Extraction: The process of driving live cartridges from the magazine into the path of the bolt or slide prior to chambering.

Extractor: The mechanical device that grabs the cartridge or shell inside a firearm.

Feeding: An element in the cycle of operation of a working firearm that loads ammunition into the breech.

Feed ramp: A slanted metal surface at the rear of a barrel that guides cartridges into the chamber during feeding.

Feet per second (FPS): A unit of measure usually used to indicate the velocity of a bullet.

Firing pin: A rod or plunger in a gun, mine, bomb, or shell that strikes and detonates a sensitive explosive to fire the main explosive or propelling charge.

Flashhole: Used in muzzle loading, this is very small hole that is open from the priming flash pan to the powder inside the barrel. Flame runs through this hole to set fire to the black powder.

Foot pounds (Ft/lbs.): A measurement of energy.

Graphite: A soft form of carbon used as a lubricant and a glaze for grains of powder to prevent the buildup of static electricity and the attendant danger of premature explosion. Also used as a flash inhibitor.

Grip adapter: A simple hard rubber, plastic, or sometimes metal filler piece that fits on a revolver between the rear of the trigger guard and the front of the grip frame to provide better support for the hand.

Grip safety: A separate mechanical safety, spring loaded and protruding from the grip or stock, usually found in an auto-loading handgun but occasionally on sub-machine and machine guns, rarely on revolvers. When at rest, a grip safety prevents firing by trigger movement but allows firing when depressed. It is located and constructed so that it is easily depressed without conscious effort when there is a normal firing grip.

Gun: A mechanism, consisting essentially of a barrel, receiver, and breech mechanism, using controlled explosives to shoot projectiles or signal flares.

Hair trigger: A trigger requiring only a light touch for firing.

Half cock: The position of the hammer of a gun when it is held by a notch in advance of the full cock position. In this position the trigger is locked, and the gun is relatively safe. The operating level which turns the cylinder when the hammer is pulled back on the receiver.

Hammer: The mechanism that strikes the firing pin or percussion cap in a firearm.

Handgun: A firearm capable of being carried and used by one hand, such as a pistol or revolver.

Hollow point: A projectile with a cavity within its point; may or may not have controlled expansion.

Hardball: A colloquial term used to describe service issue ball ammunition; usually used to describe *cartridge, ball, .45 caliber.*

Hang fire: A shot that does not fire immediately after the trigger is pulled. It does fire after a short delay. It is very dangerous. Always keep the firearm pointed in a safe direction.

Heavy slide: Addition of weight to a slide to reduce recoil while firing.

Housing: A covering or frame to protect integral parts of a firearm: i.e., a mainspring housing or trigger housing.

Immediate action: The action a person performs when a stoppage has occurred in a weapon to put the weapon back into operation with little or no loss of time.

Infrared light: Invisible light radiation of frequencies ranging beyond those of visible red. Used in firearm identification to photograph powder combustion deposits on skin and clothing not otherwise detectable.

Inside-lubricated: A bullet which is lubricated before loading. Also, a bullet that contains lubricant grooves that are not visible in the finished cartridge.

Jacket: The metal covering of a bullet.

Jerk: The effort by the shooter to fire a pistol or rifle at the precise time the sights align with the target, usually causing a bad hit on the target.

Knurl: To checker or roughen a metal surface to afford a better grip; used on pistol grips, windage screws, elevation screws, etc.

Land: The original part of the bore left after rifling grooves are formed.

Lever: A moving handle, the working of which locks or unlocks the action in guns or double rifles. There are several forms, such as top-lever, side-lever, under-lever, etc.

Lever action: A rifle whose action is operated by a lever under the stock. The lever usually serves as a trigger guard, as well as an actuating device.

Line of sight: The straight line along which sight is taken between an observer's eye and a target or other observed object or spot; specifically, the straight line between eye and target in gunnery, bombing, or rocket firing.

Locking lugs: Extension on a locking mechanism that locks the breech. Metal protuberances which form an integral part of a breech block and fit into a corresponding set of slots when the breech is closed, thus locking the gun for firing.

Magazine: Term mistakenly referred to as a clip. *(1)* Structure or compartment for storing ammunition or explosives. *(2)* That part of a gun or firearm which holds ammunition ready for chambering. **Note:** In the latter definition, magazines for small arms may be detachable or non-detachable from the rest of the piece. A box magazine is a detachable magazine in the shape of a rectangular box.

Magnum: A term used to denote a weapon of more than normal power.

Make the line safe: Command given to cause shooters to make weapons safe, to ground them, and to step back away from the firing line.

Match-conditioned weapon: Any small arm which has been made to shoot more accurately than issued or made specifically for use in competition.

Match grade: Special weapons, ammunition, or equipment manufactured for use in competitive matches.

Match-grade ammunition: Ammunition made specifically for use in competition shooting.

Match pistol: A pistol manufactured or modified to special tolerances for competitive shooting.

Maximum range: The capability of an aircraft, gun, radar transmitter, or the like that expresses the most distant point to which the aircraft can fly, the gun can shoot, etc.

Micro sight: A commercial rear sight, adjustable for windage and elevation, that can be used on almost all pistols.

Misfire: A momentary or permanent failure of a round of ammunition to fire when igniting action is taken; an instance of such failure.

National Rifle Association (NRA): An organization supported by the membership fees of millions of individual members to support and defend the rights of gun owners. (*See chapter about the NRA.*)

Nomenclature: A set or system of names or symbols

given to items of supply and equipment, to organizations, or to other variously identifiable things as a means of classification and identification.

Open sight: A rear gun sight having a notch. **Note:** Distinguished especially from a **peep sight**.

Over and under: A gun or rifle in which the barrels are placed vertically, one over the other.

Parkerize: To give a dull, relatively rough finish to a firearm by use of powered iron and phosphoric acid. Hence, *Parkerization.*

Patching: Cloth placed around the round lead ball when shooting a muzzleloader. It usually is cotton or linen.

Peep sight: A rear gun sight having a small hole in which the front sight is centered in aiming. Distinguished from an **open sight**.

Pistol: *(1)* In popular usage, a firearm, usually short-barreled, designed to be held and fired in one hand. *(2)* More precisely, such a firearm in which the chamber is an integral part of the barrel, especially a self-loading pistol, as distinguished from a revolver. *(3) A* machine pistol is usually a short-barreled weapon firing pistol ammunition in the fully automatic mode.

Pistol grip: A gunstock, the grip of which turns downward, as does a pistol's.

Projectile: An object, especially a missile, projected by an applied exterior force and continuing in motion by virtue of its own inertia, as a bullet.

Proof mark: A stamp used by gun manufacturers to identify all weapons having met the standard prescribed pressure test they consider safe. Usually found on the barrel and/or under receiver, depending on the manufacturer.

Pounds per square inch (PSI): A unit of measure used to evaluate the pressure in a chamber or cylinder.

Ramp: An inclined plane designed to give proper elevation to front or rear sights.

Ready position: The position in which a weapon is held just before aiming.

Receiver: The basic unit of firearm, especially a small arm, to which the barrel and other components are attached.

Recoil: The backward movement of a gun or part thereof on firing, caused by the backward pressure of the propellant gases; the distance that a gun or part travels in this backward movement.

Revolver: A handgun having a rotating cylinder carrying several rounds of ammunition, each round being in a chamber that comes into line with the barrel before the round is fired.

Ricochet (of a bullet, or the like): To skip, bounce, or fly off at an angle after striking an object or surface.

Rifled slug: A projectile with spiraled grooves used in shotgun ammunition, the theory being that the air forced through the grooves while the projectile is in flight tends to spin the slug to effect stability.

Rifling: *(1)* The action of cutting spiral, longitudinal grooves in the bore of a gun barrel. *(2)* The spiral grooves cut in the bore of a gun barrel or cannon.

Rim: The outer or extreme circumference on the head of a cartridge, used for head spacing in some cases, and for extraction.

Rim-fire: A cartridge in which the priming mixture is placed in the fold of the head of the shell, as in .22 caliber rim-fire cartridges.

Rimless: A cartridge case design in which the case bears no rim about the head. The extractor, in this case, will fit into an extractor groove about the head of the case.

Rimmed cartridge: A cartridge whose rim extends beyond the cartridge case to control headspace and facilitate extraction.

Ruptured cartridge: A cartridge case that is deformed, with partial or complete circumferential separation around the body.

Scatter gun/unit: Slang term for *shotgun*.

Semiautomatic: Of a firearm or gun; utilizing part of the force of an exploding cartridge to extract the empty case and chamber the next round, but requiring a separate pull on the trigger to fire each round.

Shooting eye: Refers to the dominant eye, the one used by a shooter to align his sights. The dominant eye may be identified by holding a finger at arm's length and, with both eyes open, lining it up with a distant object. If the finger remains stationary when one eye is closed, the open eye is dominant and should be used to sight a firearm.

Shooting glove: A special glove used by rifle shooters to protect the hand that is placed between the fore-end and the sling.

Shot: *(1)* Terminology applied to a fired around. *(2)* A component used in the manufacture of shot shells.

Shoulder hunch (similar to *flinch*): A reaction of the shoulder to protect the shoulder.

Side by side: A weapon with two barrels placed next to each other.

Sight alignment: When the front and rear sights are brought into correct adjustment with the eye.

Sight picture: Upon achieving proper sight alignment, a sight picture is obtained by adding the aiming area.

Silencer: A device for slowing down the escape of gases at the muzzle of a firearm, which results in the reduction of the sound of the report. It is like a muffler on an automobile. Saves hearing. It also acts as a muzzle-break and decreases the recoil of the gun. Hiram Percy Maxim developed the first successful firearm silencer in 1909. Production by Maim Silencer Company was discontinued in 1925 for lack of business. The National Firearms Act specifically includes silencers within the scope of its applications to the making and transfer of certain firearms.

Single action: *(1)* A firearm whose hammer must be cocked by hand before the weapon can be fired. *(2)* Type of fire made possible by cocking the hammer on a double-action revolver.

Skeet: A shotgun sport in which clay targets are thrown from a high house twelve feet above the ground and a low house two feet above the ground. The shooter fires from eight different positions, which are laid out on a semicircle, with the eighth position at the center of the diameter of the semicircle. A round of skeet consists of twenty-five shots, with the maximum of twenty-five points.

Sling: A leather or web strap used to help support a rifle during firing.

Small of stock: A name usually applied to the *hand* of the butt stock. Commonly called the **pistol grip**.

Smallbore: Normally refers to a .22 caliber rim fire cartridge or weapons chambered for such cartridges.

Terminal velocity: The constant velocity of a falling body attained when the resistance of air or ambient fluid has become equal to the force of gravity acting upon the body.

Tracer: *(1)* A projectile that has a chemical compound which gives a trail of light indicating the flight of the projectile. *(2)* The pyrotechnic composition in a bullet.

Trajectory: The curve on the vertical lane traced by a bullet or other object thrown, launched, or projected by an applied exterior force, the projectile continuing in motion after separation from the force.

Trap: A shotgun sport in which clay targets are thrown at a fixed height with an angle of 130 degrees. The trap house is located sixteen feet from each of the five positions from which the shooter fires five shots, giving a maximum score of twenty-five points.

Triangulation: A sighting and aiming exercise.

Trigger: A mechanism which, when pulled with the finger, releases another mechanism, as in the trigger of a gun.

Trigger control: The ability to move the trigger until the sear disengages, the hammer goes forward, and the weapon discharges, without any movement of the weapon.

Trigger pull: *(1)* The amount of weight necessary to actuate the trigger. *(2)* The length of the trigger travel during actuation.

Trigger shoe: A device designed for widening the trigger.

Trigger squeeze: The speed or rate of motion in a given direction and in a given frame of reference.

Trigger stop: Prevents excessive rearward travel of the trigger after sear/striker release.

Twist Velocity: The distance in inches that a bullet travels through the barrel to make one complete revolution.

Ventilated rib: A strip of metal, usually steel, running the full length of a shotgun barrel with rectangular holes evenly spaced to help eliminate heat waves from the line of sight and produce a flat sighting plane.

Wadcutter: A term used to describe a lead bullet, which cuts cleanly through the target upon impact. Cartridges containing these bullets usually have a reduced load.

Made in the USA
Middletown, DE
08 March 2021

35065593R00106